The Gilded Age Christmas Cookbook

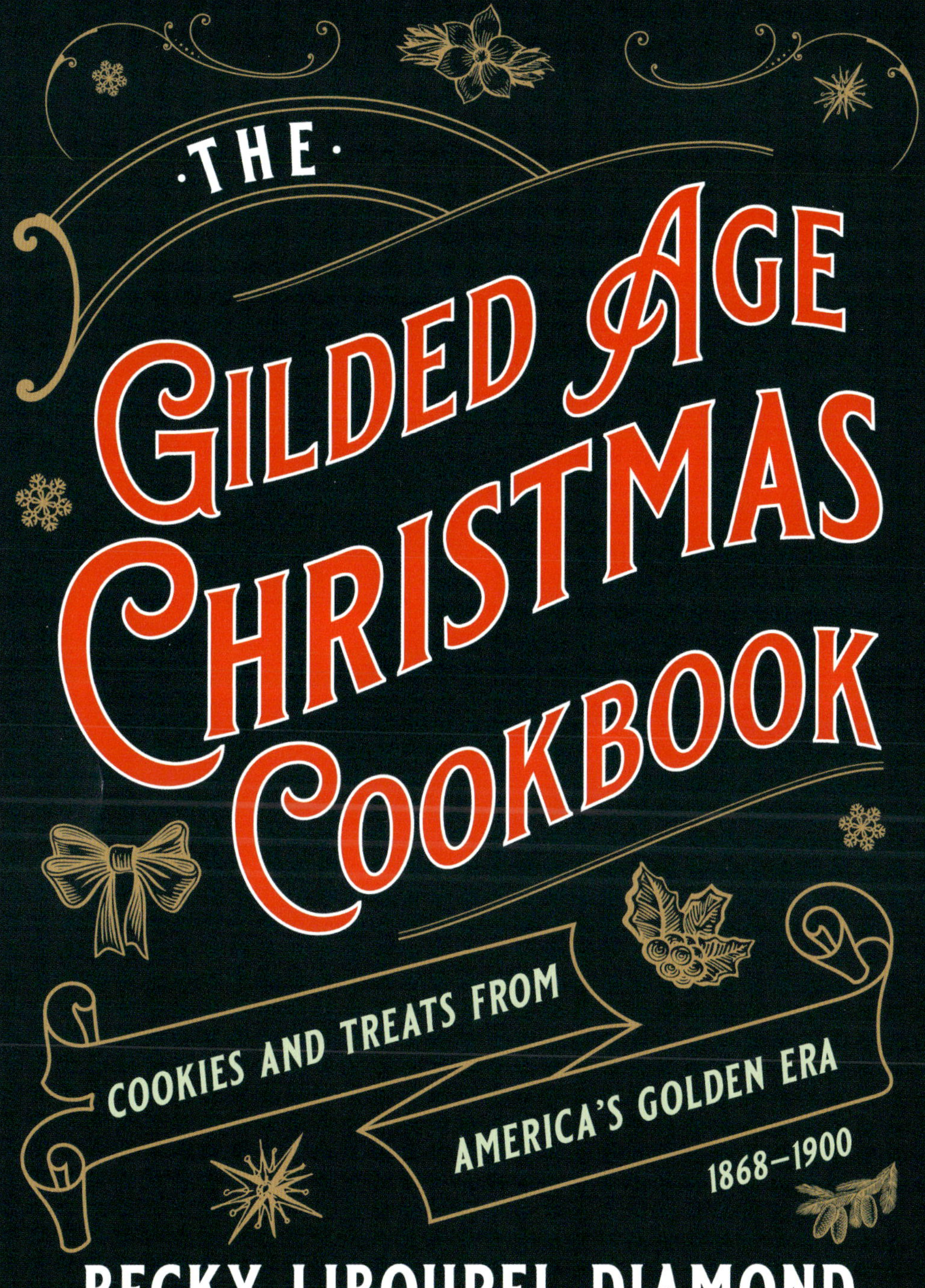

THE GILDED AGE CHRISTMAS COOKBOOK

COOKIES AND TREATS FROM AMERICA'S GOLDEN ERA 1868–1900

BECKY LIBOUREL DIAMOND

Globe Pequot
Essex, Connecticut

Globe
Pequot

An imprint of The Globe Pequot Publishing Group, Inc.
64 South Main Street
Essex, CT 06426
www.globepequot.com

Distributed by NATIONAL BOOK NETWORK

British Library Cataloguing in Publication Information available

Library of Congress Cataloging-in-Publication Data
Names: Diamond, Becky Libourel, author. | Raub, Heather, photographer. | Staib, Walter, writer of foreword.
Title: The Gilded Age Christmas cookbook : cookies and treats from America's golden era / Becky Libourel Diamond ; photography by Heather Raub of FrontRoom Images ; foreword by chef Walter Staib.
Description: Essex, Connecticut : Globe Pequot, [2025] | Includes bibliographical references and index. | Summary: "With origins dating to the nineteenth century and even earlier, the recipes in this book have been adapted for today's ingredients and appliances, allowing cooks to re-create them in their own modern kitchens. Each recipe features the fascinating history behind each cookie, its ingredients, and baking methods"— Provided by publisher.
Identifiers: LCCN 2025000947 (print) | LCCN 2025000948 (ebook) | ISBN 9781493088423 (cloth) | ISBN 9781493088430 (epub)
Subjects: LCSH: Christmas cooking. | Desserts. | Baking—United States—History—19th century. | LCGFT: Cookbooks.
Classification: LCC TX739.2.C45 D523 2025 (print) | LCC TX739.2.C45 (ebook) | DDC 641.5/6860973—dc23/eng/20250227
LC record available at https://lccn.loc.gov/2025000947
LC ebook record available at https://lccn.loc.gov/2025000948

♾™ The paper used in this publication meets the minimum requirements of American National Standard for Information Sciences—Permanence of Paper for Printed Library Materials, ANSI/NISO Z39.48-1992.

For my parents,
who always made Christmas special

Contents

FOREWORD

There's something undeniably magical about Christmas: the festive spirit, the glittering decorations, the warmth of family gatherings, and of course, the mouthwatering aromas wafting from the kitchen, where the season's sweetest treats are lovingly prepared. For me, this magic is deeply connected to the cherished culinary traditions passed down through generations, particularly those of my German heritage. When Becky Libourel Diamond approached me to write the foreword for her latest book, *The Gilded Age Christmas Cookbook: Cookies and Treats from America's Golden Era*, I was immediately transported back to those nostalgic flavors and the holiday joy they evoke.

My journey into the culinary world began in the Black Forest of Germany, where I was practically raised in the kitchen. From a young age, I found myself surrounded by the smells and sounds of my uncle's restaurant, Gasthaus Zum Buckenberg. My first "job" was peeling garlic, but I was always drawn to the sweeter side of the kitchen, where my mother and grandmother would craft the most delightful cookies, cakes, and pastries. These early experiences left a lifelong mark on me, shaping not just my career but also my appreciation for the traditions that make food so much more than just sustenance.

In the eighteenth century, long before America's Gilded Age, German immigrants brought with them a wealth of culinary knowledge and traditions. Among these were their cherished recipes for cookies, which would later evolve and blend with other European influences in the melting pot of early America. The Pennsylvania Germans, or "Pennsylvania Dutch," were particularly known for their baked goods, especially during the holiday season. Their recipes for spiced cookies like lebkuchen and springerle, with their rich flavors and intricate designs, became staples in many American households.

By the time the Gilded Age rolled around in the late nineteenth century, these German influences had become deeply ingrained in American holiday traditions. The Gilded Age was a period of great affluence and opulence,

in which American society indulged in the finest things life had to offer, and this extravagance extended to their Christmas celebrations. During this era, cookies and other treats were not just simple sweets; they were symbols of wealth, status, and the cultural exchange of early America. The elaborate cookie recipes and desserts enjoyed during this time were often a reflection of the diverse European heritages of the American elite, with German baking playing a starring role.

German bakers, with their meticulous techniques and a deep respect for tradition, were highly regarded for their contributions to Victorian-era desserts. Their influence is particularly evident in the array of Christmas cookies that became popular during the Gilded Age. From pfeffernüsse, the tiny, spiced, sugar-dusted cookies, to the buttery, nutty flavors of vanillekipferl, these treats added a touch of Old World charm to American Christmas tables. These recipes were often passed down through generations, each family adding their own twist, and they became a cherished part of the American Christmas culinary landscape.

Becky Libourel Diamond has masterfully captured this rich history in her new book, taking readers on a journey through the Gilded Age, where the cookie was much more than a simple baked good—it was a piece of history, a symbol of the blending of cultures, and a testament to the evolving American identity. Her extensive research and deep understanding of this era bring to life the stories behind the recipes, offering readers not just a cookbook, but a portal to the past.

What I love most about Becky's work is her ability to connect the dots between history, culture, and food in such a relatable and engaging way. She has an extraordinary talent for making history feel alive and relevant, and this book is no exception. Through her careful curation of recipes, she invites us to experience the opulence and tradition of the Gilded Age, while also offering a glimpse into the lives of the people who shaped America's culinary heritage.

Becky and I share a deep appreciation for the stories that food can tell. In my own work, both at City Tavern and through my television series, *A Taste of History*, I've always been passionate about exploring the connections between food and history, showing how what we eat is a reflection of who we are and where we come from. It's a passion that Becky clearly shares, and it's one of the reasons I've been so thrilled to support her work over the years.

Her new book is a treasure trove of recipes and stories that will transport you back to a time of grand holiday celebrations, where every cookie was crafted with care and every bite was a taste of history. Whether you're a seasoned baker looking to expand your repertoire or simply someone who loves the idea of bringing a bit of the past into your present-day celebrations, this book has something for you.

As you embark on your journey through *The Gilded Age Christmas Cookbook*, I encourage you to take your time, savor the stories, and most importantly, enjoy the process of baking these incredible treats. After all, the holiday season is about more than just the end result—it's about the joy of creation, the warmth of sharing, and the memories we make along the way.

So, tie on your apron, preheat your oven, and get ready to take a delicious trip back to America's Gilded Age. You're in for a treat!

Chef Walter Staib
host/executive producer, *A Taste of History*
president, Concepts by Staib, Ltd.
former proprietor, City Tavern Restaurant

TIPS ON INGREDIENTS AND TECHNIQUES

Several recipes in this cookbook call for ground nutmeg. If you can, purchase a jar of whole nutmegs and grate them with a fine grater yourself as you need them. The spice will be much fresher tasting!

Rosewater and orange flower water (sometimes called orange blossom water) can be found online or in specialty markets like Whole Foods and sometimes the international section of supermarkets. I usually use Al Wadi brand (Cortas and Sadaf are other brands).

Citron was a common ingredient in many Gilded Age Christmas desserts and is included in a few recipes in this cookbook. Diced candied citron can be found in the baking section of many grocery stores or online. Paradise is a brand commonly used.

Superfine granulated sugar is included in a couple of recipes in this cookbook. It can be found in many grocery stores under the Domino brand, but if you can't find it, simply process granulated sugar for one minute in a food processor or blender.

WHIPPING EGG WHITES

Room-temperature eggs will whip easier, so for best results separate eggs when they are cold and then let them come to room temperature, about thirty minutes. Always use a clean mixing bowl made from glass, stainless steel, or copper (not plastic). When whipping egg whites with an electric mixer, start on a low speed and then increase speed when they start to look foamy. The length of time depends on the stage you need for the recipe as well as other factors including the age of the eggs and the temperature and humidity of your kitchen. Use this sight guide to help:

- **FOAMY** The egg whites will look foamy with small bubbles. At this point, some recipes call for cream of tartar or another acidic ingredient to help boost volume.
- **SOFT PEAKS** The egg whites hold their shape and droop over to the side when the beater is lifted up. If making a meringue or another sweet recipe, this is the stage to add the sugar.
- **FIRM PEAKS** The egg whites will keep their shape when the beater is lifted up.
- **STIFF PEAKS** The tips of the egg whites will look smooth and glossy and stand straight up both on the beater(s) and on the surface.

For those leery of using raw egg whites in any of the icing recipes, you can substitute ¼ cup meringue powder and ½ cup cold water for the fresh egg whites. To substitute for 1 egg white, you can mix 2 teaspoons meringue powder with 2 tablespoons water.

MAKING WHIPPED CREAM

A chilled bowl and beater(s) will make whipping cream quicker and more efficient, so when making whipped cream, it's best to put the mixing bowl and beater(s) in the freezer for at least fifteen minutes.

PIE CRUSTS

The recipes in this book are for all-butter pie crusts. Feel free to use your own favorite pie crust recipe or purchase premade pie crusts instead.

RECREATING RECIPES

In order to be authentic to the Gilded Age, dozens of cookbooks, newspapers, magazines, and personal accounts from the era were consulted to produce this cookbook. The end result is a series of recipes that have been recreated to reflect modern ingredients and equipment and are not overly complicated for home cooks to replicate in their own kitchens.

LYNDHURST MANSION, TARRYTOWN, NY

HOSTING YOUR OWN GILDED AGE–THEMED HOLIDAY CELEBRATION

Don't worry if you don't have access to authentic Gilded Age dishes, glassware, and serving pieces. Mix and match family heirlooms and vintage items from yard sales, thrift stores, etc., or simply use whatever you have and make it your own! Just like the phrase "'tis the season," holiday gatherings are all about spreading good cheer among family and friends.

LYNDHURST MANSION, TARRYTOWN, NY

INTRODUCTION

The children were nestled all snug in their beds;
While visions of sugar-plums danced in their heads.

These two lines from Clement Clarke Moore's famous poem "A Visit from St. Nicholas" perfectly capture the magical charm and special treats associated with Christmas. Although most Americans have heard of sugar plums thanks to this often-recited holiday favorite, many have likely never have had the pleasure of tasting one of these luxuries or even know what they really are (hint: they are not sugar-dusted plums).

This is because sugar plums are one of the Gilded Age–era holiday sweets that got eclipsed as America moved into the twentieth century. But *The Gilded Age Christmas Cookbook* bridges the past and present, bringing back sugar plums and other confections not typically found in modern cookbooks, while revisiting some beloved favorites. Whisking readers back in time to this fanciful era, the treats will delight the inner child in everyone.

During the Gilded Age (1868–1900), many of the Christmas traditions still celebrated today in America began to become mainstream. People from countries all over the world brought their various customs with them to America. As a result, the celebration of Christmas in the United States ended up being a mix of different traditions from several nations. The biggest influence stemmed from the influx of immigrants who came from places in Europe such as Germany, England, the Netherlands, Central Europe, and Scandinavia, who brought their Christmas rituals and celebrations with them. This included putting up and decorating a Christmas tree, hanging up stockings so they could be filled with treats, the legend of gift giver St. Nicholas (who became Santa Claus in America), and of course baking and enjoying Christmas cookies and other sweets.

The concept of eating tasty sugary foods to mark significant occasions can actually be traced back to ancient times. Cultures from all over the world enjoyed sweet treats such as cakes, cookies, and candies as part of festive holiday rituals long before people began celebrating Christmas. Many of these recipes and their ingredients, such as cinnamon, ginger, black pepper, almonds, and dried fruits, were introduced to Europe in the Middle Ages. Highly valued, they were quickly incorporated into European baked goods and subsequently made their way to America.

These spices and dried fruits found their way into a variety of Christmas cookies, which were very much a part of Gilded Age holiday celebrations. Abundant amounts of Christmas cookies were baked to give as gifts, hang up as decorations to adorn windows and Christmas trees, or just to have on hand as a hospitable treat when company called. Cookie cutters and decorative molds (such as those used for New Year's cookies and springerle) were introduced to America by Dutch and German settlers.

Mincemeat pies and plum pudding were other popular Christmas treats that incorporated many of these spices and dried fruits. Traditional British desserts, they were the highlight of Gilded Age holiday tables in America. In fact, many Christmas menus (especially those from earlier in the era) listed *only* these two items as desserts. But by the latter part of the nineteenth century, other festive desserts began to crop up, especially on holiday menus that were multi-course, perhaps to mirror the excess that was so common during the period. These included indulgences such as cakes, puddings, tarts, and candies.

During the Gilded Age it was popular for holiday celebrations to continue through New Year's Day and even into Twelfth Night (January 6). So although the focus of this cookbook is on Christmas desserts and treats, a sampling of sweet dishes enjoyed in the week or two after Christmas is also featured, as well as an example of treats served to commemorate the Jewish holiday of Hanukkah, also celebrated in December.

With origins that date back to the nineteenth century and even earlier, the recipes in *The Gilded Age Christmas Cookbook* have been adapted for today's ingredients and appliances, allowing cooks to recreate them in their own modern kitchens. Each recipe provides a colorful glimpse into the Gilded Age era, featuring the fascinating history behind each sweet treat, its ingredients, and baking methods. I hope you enjoy this festive taste of the Gilded Age!

MARK TWAIN'S CHRISTMAS STORIES

Author and satirist Mark Twain will be forever identified with the Gilded Age, a tongue-in-cheek expression he coined in his 1873 novel of the same name. Never one to mince words, Twain did not shy away from writing and lecturing about the era's political, economic, and social issues with his distinctive comedic edge. Twain is also associated with the Christmas season through his writings, many of which provide firsthand accounts of how the holiday season was viewed and celebrated during the Gilded Age.

For example, one of Twain's early stories, "The Christmas Fireside: The Story of the Bad Little Boy That Bore a Charmed Life," was published in the newly launched literary weekly *The Californian* on December 23, 1865. Its main character, Jim, is familiar to readers of Twain: a mischievous, Tom Sawyer type of boy who grows up to be a man with few morals. The acerbic theme conveyed by Twain in this piece aligns with the era's mindset of permitting (and even rewarding) cheating and corruption in business and politics.

Twain continued to mock Gilded Age excesses in other holiday-themed writings, exemplified by this quote from his 1897 travelogue, *Following the Equator*: "The approach of Christmas brings harassment and dread to many excellent people. They have to buy a cart-load of presents, and they never know what to buy to hit the various tastes; they put in three weeks of hard and anxious work, and when Christmas morning comes they are so dissatisfied with the result, and so disappointed that they want to sit down and cry. Then they give thanks that Christmas comes but once a year."

But Twain actually succumbed to the season and its charms, bringing his personal feelings of the holiday into his writing, especially the many joyful Christmases he spent with his family. As Carlo DeVito notes in *A Mark Twain*

Christmas, "Twain loved the Christmas season, and reveled in its luxuries as much as its obvious foibles." He adored his wife Livy, and both of them were generous with each other and their children, especially at Christmas. They were also charitable with the poor, keeping gift baskets near the foyer to be given out on Christmas Eve.

The entire Twain house was festive with holiday décor, with boughs of pine-scented greenery adorning the fireplace mantle and framing doorways. Their Christmas tree was decked out with sparkling tinsel and paper ornaments; crocheted snowflakes; and strings of popcorn and cranberries handmade by the couple's three daughters, Susy, Clara, and Jean. The family loved to sit around the piano and sing Christmas carols and hymns. Twain's daughter Clara recalled hanging up stockings on Christmas Eve and listening to her mother read "A Visit from St. Nicholas." Sometimes Twain would even delight the girls by dressing up as Santa Claus and recounting his journeys around the world delivering gifts. It was a warm and cozy holiday setting.

Twain's love for his family and the Christmas season was probably best demonstrated in "A Letter from Santa Claus," penned in 1875 for his young daughter, Susy, to find on her pillow on Christmas morning. Referencing the Christmas gift wish lists sent to Santa by Susy and Clara, it is written in a delightful, playful tone accompanied by Twain's signature wit. Signed "Your loving Santa Claus," it was a comforting reminder that Santa is a kind and joyful presence—not only at Christmastime, but throughout the year.

Chapter One
Cookies

SPICE COOKIES

Spice Nuts
Soft Molasses Cookies
Coffee Cookies
Gingerbread Cookies

SUGAR COOKIES

Sparkly Sugar Christmas Cookies
Frosted Christmas Cookies
Sand Tarts
Brown Sugar Cookies
Holiday Jumbles

BUTTER COOKIES

Scotch Shortbread
German Butter Cookies
Galettes
Apricot Tea Cookies

In filling the Christmas stockings use the cakes and cookies in place of the bonbons and the children will be all the happier next day.

—SARA SEDGWICK, *THE INDEPENDENT*, 1891

MANY OF THE EARLIEST Christmas cookies were a form of gingerbread, such as German lebkuchen. The texture and shape of the cookies varied depending on the region they in which they originated. Some were sweetened with honey, others with brown sugar, molasses (also called treacle), and/or golden syrup (both by-products of the sugar refining process). According to food historian Will Weaver, those that used honey came from middle European countries (such as Germany), and those that were molasses based originated in England or Scotland. Some recipes resulted in a cookie that was crisp and snappy; others were softer and thicker. Christmas sugar cookie recipes typically stemmed from English traditions.

Just like today, cookie baking started weeks before Christmas. Many recipes yielded dozens of cookies in a single batch, some as large as a small plate, six to eight inches across. The reasons cookies were made by the "washbasketful" was so there would be plenty on hand for a number of occasions: Belsnickeling (a custom carried over from Germany in which groups of masked youths would go from house to house on Christmas Eve to entertain and sing to people in return for goodies or small coins, which could amount to forty to fifty people "dropping by"), to give as gifts, to decorate the Christmas tree, to tuck into Christmas stockings, and to display in downstairs windows to greet those passing by.

One difference was in the holiday cookie shapes that were typical of cutout cookies during the Gilded Age. Made of tin, Christmas cookie cutters were often in the shape of animals, both the domesticated variety such as dogs, cats, horses, chickens, fish, and rabbits, as well as more exotic ones such as elephants, deer, and tigers. Other popular shapes included hearts, diamonds, leaves, and flowers. There were even larger cookie cutters that made several small cookies at once to serve as Christmas tree decorations.

So although some of the cookies featured here predate the Gilded Age in terms of when they originated, all were beloved as part of Christmas festivities during the era.

SPICE COOKIES

Today we often associate gingerbread men or spice cookies with Christmas, as was also the case in the Gilded Age. These cookies, or "cakes" as they were originally called, could be seasoned with a variety of spices, including nutmeg, allspice, ginger, cloves, and cinnamon, as well as ground caraway, anise or coriander seeds, and even black or red pepper. Many of these were traditional Christmas treats brought to America by European immigrants.

For example, pfeffernüsse are traditional European Christmas cookies that have a great number of variations depending on where they are from. *Pfeffernüsse* is the German name, but they are also known as *pepernoten* in Dutch, *pebernødder* in Danish, *pepparnoter* in Swedish, and *peppernuts* in English (which is the literal translation). The "pepper" refers to the tiny bit of black pepper that is added along with cinnamon, nutmeg, and allspice. But the "nut" part of the name does not mean the cookies contained nuts. It was more a reference to the fact that the cookies were roughly the size of nuts and could be eaten by the handful.

Many spice cookies also used molasses in place of some (or all) of the sugar. Molasses first made its way to America from the Caribbean as a by-product of the process of refining sugarcane and quickly became a popular sweetener for cooking and baking, particularly since it was less expensive than refined white sugar. As a quicker mixing method, the butter or lard was heated in the molasses before the remaining ingredients were added. The look and texture of spice cookies were as diverse as the ingredients. Some were soft and chewy, and others were thin and crisp. In addition to the small nut shape, spice cookies were also baked as little individual cakes, rolled out into ropes and then formed into circles, or rolled very thin and then cut out with a cookie cutter. The term "ginger snaps" was introduced around 1805. "Snap" came from the Dutch word *snappen*, meaning "to seize quickly." These hard, crunchy cookies were often made with blackstrap molasses and tended to "snap the teeth."

Spice Nuts

Spice nuts do not contain nuts but instead refer to the fact that the cookies are tiny, about the size of nuts. Other names for this cookie have included cobblestones, German Christmas cakes, and ginger nuts. The version below is adapted from Mrs. Elizabeth Goodfellow, a Philadelphia pastry shop proprietress who ran a cooking school and catering business in the early 1800s.

MAKES ABOUT 4 DOZEN COOKIES

½ stick (4 tablespoons) butter
1 cup molasses
4 tablespoons sugar
1 teaspoon ground ginger
1 teaspoon ground cinnamon
1 teaspoon allspice
1 tablespoon baking soda
⅓ cup finely chopped crystallized ginger
3 cups all-purpose flour

Preheat the oven to 350°F. Line baking sheets with parchment paper.

Place the butter and molasses in a large saucepan and warm over low heat. When the butter is melted, add sugar, spices, baking soda, and crystallized ginger.

Stir until well mixed and then remove the pan from the stove. Add the flour one cup at a time, mixing well after each addition, until a soft dough is formed.

Taking a softball-sized lump at a time, roll out onto a floured surface into a 1-inch-wide rope shape. If the dough is sticky, add flour in small increments to make it easier to work with.

Cut the rope into 1-inch pieces and place about 1 inch apart on baking sheet. Alternatively, roll small pieces of the dough into little balls and place about 1 inch apart on the baking sheet.

Bake for 10–12 minutes. Transfer from baking sheet to a wire rack and let cool completely.

Soft Molasses Cookies

This recipe, which comes from my grandfather's mother, May Belle Patterson, evokes cookies typical of the Gilded Age in that it makes a huge number, enough for having on hand for holiday guests, a cookie exchange, or any holiday event at which a sizable number of cookies are required. You will need a very large mixing bowl and might have to mix in the flour by hand if you feel your electric mixer is straining a bit to mix this large amount of dough. And feel free to enlist the help of family members to roll them out. You will be rewarded with dozens of big, soft, cake-like molasses cookies!

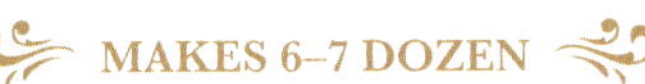

MAKES 6–7 DOZEN

1 cup sugar
2 sticks (1 cup) unsalted butter, softened
1 egg, beaten
1 cup molasses
8 cups flour
2 teaspoons baking soda
½ teaspoon salt
2 teaspoons ginger
1 teaspoon cinnamon
1 cup buttermilk
Confectioners' sugar (optional)

Preheat oven to 375°F. Line baking sheets with parchment paper.

Using an electric mixer, beat sugar and butter until creamy. Add egg and molasses and continue mixing until combined. In a separate bowl, sift the flour with the baking soda, salt, ginger, and cinnamon. Add to the wet ingredients alternately with the buttermilk.

Roll dough out on a floured surface and cut into shapes with cookie cutters. (If dough is sticky, add up to ¼ cup more flour in small increments.)

Place about 2 inches apart on baking sheets and bake for 10–12 minutes or until nicely browned. Cookies will puff up nicely and have a soft texture. Transfer from baking sheet to wire rack, let cool completely, and sprinkle with confectioners' sugar or decorate with royal icing.

Soft Molasses Cookies

CONTINUED

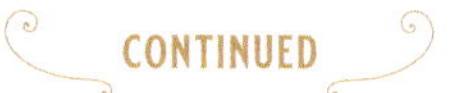

ROYAL ICING

2 egg whites

2 teaspoons lemon juice

3¼ cups confectioners' sugar, sifted

Whisk egg whites in a bowl on low speed until foamy, about 4–5 minutes, then stir in lemon juice. Add confectioners' sugar a little at a time, increasing speed to medium-high until icing is smooth and glossy.

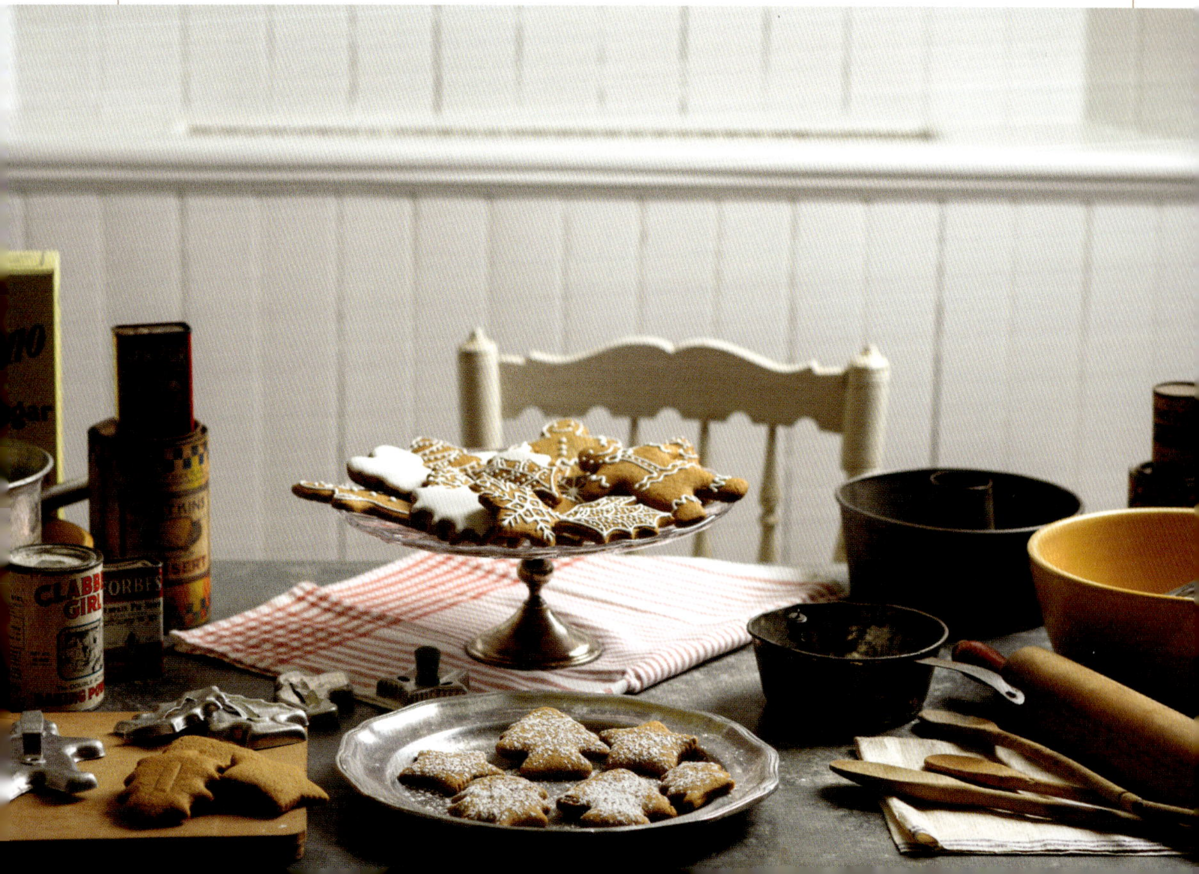

Santa Claus

It was during the Gilded Age that Santa Claus as we know him today, with his fur-trimmed red suit, pack of toys, reindeer, sleigh, and home at the North Pole, became a central part of Christmas in America. This image was introduced by *Harper's Weekly* illustrator Thomas Nast, who published a series of prints depicting Santa Claus from 1863 through 1886. (Nast was also the political cartoonist who came up with the representation of an elephant for the Republican Party and a donkey for the Democratic Party and exposed corruption by Tammany Hall within New York's mayoral office.)

Stocking of Contents, wood engraving by Thomas Nast, 1890. LIBRARY OF CONGRESS

SANTA CLAUS

CONTINUED

At first, Nast drew Santa as elf sized, wearing a fur jumpsuit and a little round hat, a beard, and whiskers. In fact, a two-page spread called "Santa Claus and His Works," published in *Harper's Weekly* in 1866, depicted a diminutive Santa making presents in his workshop. He was so tiny he could barely peer into his book of "naughty and nice"

Caught, wood engraving by Thomas Nast, 1889. LIBRARY OF CONGRESS

names (also a Nast creation). Eventually, Nast settled on characterizing him as a life-sized, portly old man with a long white beard and a pipe. This description seized the public's imagination and has become part of Santa's official image ever since.

We also have Nast to thank for selecting the North Pole as Santa's home address. One of his 1882 drawings portrayed the jolly gift giver perched on top of a crate with the label "Christmas box 1882, St. Nicholas, North Pole." Allegedly Nast's inspiration came from Clement C. Moore's poem "A Visit from St. Nicholas." Writing on a frigid December evening in 1822 in New York's Greenwich Village, Moore was apparently on a sleigh ride to pick up a turkey his wife wished to cook for the poor when he conceived the poem as a way to entertain his wife and six children when he got home. Although the poem was first published anonymously (supposedly without his permission) in New York's *Troy Sentinel* in 1823, Moore (a professor of classical literature) did not formally acknowledge writing the poem until 1837, when it was published in *The New York Book of Poetry*.

The vivid descriptions of St. Nicholas in this famous poem kicked off the visual imagery of Santa Claus that continued throughout the century, particularly the line "He was dressed all in fur, from his head to his foot," which increased the likelihood that St. Nick came from a cold climate. By the Gilded Age, the image of a chubby, red-cheeked, fur-robed, white-bearded Santa driving a sleigh led by eight flying reindeer delivering toys made in his North Pole workshop was embedded in American Christmas lore.

Coffee Cookies

Think of these soft, chewy cookies as "molasses cookies with a kick." Featured in an early 1900s Ladies Home Journal *article titled "Some Good Christmas Cookies," by Mrs. Sarah Tyson Rorer (a well-known Gilded Age cooking instructor from Philadelphia), the original recipe called for a "pint of strong, warm coffee." Since that much coffee would not work in a modern cookie dough, I used a combination of brewed coffee and instant coffee (which was just entering the marketplace in the early 1900s). The addition of ginger gives these cookies a tinge of spiciness.*

MAKES ABOUT 3½ DOZEN COOKIES

- 1 stick (½ cup) salted butter, softened
- ¾ cup sugar
- ¼ cup molasses
- ¼ cup strong brewed coffee
- 2¾ cups all-purpose flour
- 1 teaspoon baking soda
- ½ teaspoon ginger
- 2 tablespoons instant coffee (I used Starbucks premium instant dark roast)
- Additional granulated sugar, for rolling

Preheat oven to 350°F. Line baking sheets with parchment paper.

Using an electric mixer, cream butter and sugar in a bowl on medium-high speed. Turn down to low and add molasses and coffee.

In a large bowl, mix flour, baking soda, ginger, and instant coffee. Add to the butter, sugar, and molasses mixture and mix until ingredients form a soft dough. Gather dough into a ball, wrap in plastic wrap, and chill in the refrigerator for at least 1 hour.

Scoop dough into walnut-sized balls and roll in granulated sugar. Place about 2 inches apart on baking sheets and bake for 10–12 minutes. Cookies will still be slightly soft but will harden as they cool. Allow to cool on baking sheets for a few minutes, then remove to a wire rack and let cool completely.

Gingerbread Cookies

Ingwer Gebäck

Like gingerbread and lebkuchen, gingerbread cookies were a staple in my home, especially around the holidays. Christmas just wouldn't have been the same without rolling out the dough, cutting it into fanciful shapes, and filling the house with the scent of sweet spiciness. This recipe relies on the bold, pungent flavors of a variety of spices and a handful of sweeteners, including brown and granulated sugars, apple cider, molasses, honey, and maple syrup, all of which give the cookies a rich and pleasantly balanced sweetness.

MAKES ABOUT 16 COOKIES

6¼ cups all-purpose flour
2¼ teaspoons baking soda
1 tablespoon ground ginger
1 teaspoon ground allspice
½ teaspoon ground cloves
½ teaspoon freshly grated nutmeg
½ teaspoon ground cardamom
⅛ teaspoon ground mace
¾ cup apple cider
½ cup dark molasses
¼ cup honey
¼ cup maple syrup
1 stick (½ cup) unsalted butter, softened
¼ cup dark brown sugar
¼ cup granulated sugar
2 tablespoons chopped fresh ginger

Sift together the flour, baking soda, and spices in a large bowl. Stir together the cider, molasses, honey, and maple syrup in a medium bowl.

Place the butter in the bowl of an electric stand mixer fitted with the paddle attachment and begin mixing on medium speed. While mixing, add the sugars and ginger; continue mixing until light and fluffy, stopping at least once to scrape down the sides of the bowl.

Continuing to mix on medium speed, gradually add the wet ingredients to the butter and sugar, pouring in a thin steady stream and stopping once to scrape down the sides of the bowl. Reduce the mixing speed to low and gradually add the dry ingredients, mixing just until combined. Wrap the dough in plastic wrap and chill in the refrigerator for about 1 hour.

Preheat the oven to 375°F and line baking sheets with parchment paper.

Gingerbread Cookies

Working with about one-quarter of the dough at a time, place it on a lightly floured work surface and roll to ¼ inch thick. Cut into desired shapes, arrange the cookies about 2 inches apart on the baking sheets, and bake until they have lightened in color, about 12–15 minutes. Transfer the cookies to wire racks and let cool completely, Store in airtight containers.

Excerpt from Walter Staib, Black Forest Cuisine Cookbook *(Philadelphia: Running Press, 2006)*

Cookies for Santa

Today the last thing many American children do before scampering up to bed on Christmas Eve is leave a plate of cookies and a glass of milk for Santa (and perhaps a few carrots for his reindeer). Although this holiday tradition didn't really kick off until the 1930s (during the Great Depression, when parents were trying to teach children a lesson in gratitude), the kernel of the idea was there before that. Centuries earlier, Dutch children began leaving out a shoe containing a carrot or some hay and a bowl of water for the large white horse ridden by Sinterklaas (St. Nicholas) as he made his way through the night delivering gifts on December 5.

Although I wasn't able to find many Gilded Age references to leaving cookies for Santa, I did track down a letter to the editor printed in *St. Nicholas* magazine in 1896 written by a twelve-year-old girl named Anna from Coronado, California, relaying the story of a "Christmas Cabin" her family had set up the prior year in place of a Christmas tree. Positioned in front of their fireplace (so the stockings could still be hung from the mantel), it had a sloping roof made from white cloth and was decorated with popcorn strings, greenery, and ribbons. While their parents were setting it up, Anna's three-year-old brother Edwin suggested putting out a little table for Santa with some lunch on it "because he will be hungry." When the children's father asked what type of food they should put out, the little boy said, "a glass of milk and some cookies." Just like today, the father ate the cookies and drank the milk after the boy went to bed, although when little Edwin came down in the morning and saw the empty plate and glass, he was convinced Santa had indeed consumed the treats, saying "Santa Claus will have to come back and eat the rest of the cookies."

Merry Christmas holiday postcard. NEW YORK PUBLIC LIBRARY DIGITAL COLLECTIONS

Dressing up as Santa

Just as we do today, Gilded Age folks thought it was great fun to dress up as Santa Claus to give joy to little ones in the family. The chosen volunteer (typically a man or older boy) would dress in a thick fur coat, cap, and gloves, stuffed with pillows to give the appearance of being plump and jolly. A muffler would cover most of Santa's face so that only his eyes and nose were visible, and his nose and cheeks were colored red with carmine (see Colorants sidebar on page 24).

There were a variety of ways those playing Santa Claus would enter the room. One way was to rattle a string of sleigh bells outside, first very softly and then increasingly louder to simulate Santa's sleigh approaching. Santa would then shout, "Whoa!" and enter the house through a window or the door. To pretend Santa was coming down the chimney, some families would place a wooden fireplace mantel in front of a door and cover the upper part of the doorway with cloth to look like the mantelpiece. Santa could then safely enter the room through the "fireplace" without actually having to climb inside the chimney. To replicate Santa descending from the roof, a chair was placed behind one side of a doorway so that Santa could step down from it and appear to be coming down from the rooftop. Sometimes the pretend Santa either carried the presents in a sack or retrieved them from the "chimney" replica or from where they were arranged on the Christmas tree. He also often crammed presents into large stockings hung on either side of the imitation mantel, which were then taken out by someone else and distributed. The person playing Santa spoke in a deep voice as he handed out the presents, making remarks appropriate to each gift in turn.

SUGAR COOKIES

In early America, cookies were often considered a special treat because sugar (particularly white sugar, the most refined variety) and other sweeteners were expensive and/or difficult to obtain. Historically, white sugar has been the most desirable for baked goods, and therefore the costliest, typically reserved for the well-to-do. By the beginning of the 1800s, large-scale sugar production had become possible through the horrific and unfortunate spread of enslaved labor in the Caribbean, and by the 1820s most Americans were well acquainted with sugar, although it was still considered a luxury item for most.

It was around this time that the term *granulated sugar* also came into use, due to changes in the way sugar was stored and shipped. Prior to this, white sugar was sold in hard molded loaves or cones. Pieces of sugar were pinched off with iron sugar nippers (a kitchen tool resembling a pair of pliers) and pounded in a mortar and pestle to achieve the desired consistency. In the 1850s, the Boston Sugar Refinery began developing granulated sugar as a replacement for sugar cones. Sugar was dried on a large table by wooden rakes and then separated by mesh sieves into coarse and fine grades of sugar and packaged and sold accordingly. Powdered (or confectioners') sugar was typically manufactured from the coarsest granulated sugar after it was thoroughly cooled.

Additional sugar processing improvements continued throughout the nineteenth century, and this, combined with the development of beet sugar, increased the supply and lowered costs. By the 1880s, sugar became a more affordable commodity and sugar prices continued their steady decline, allowing those in the middle and lower classes to indulge in confections, particularly for special celebrations such as Christmas.

Many types of Christmas cookies obtained their sweetness from brown sugar, which was typically lower in price and coarser grained, taking its color, flavor, and texture from molasses syrup present during the refining process. As Mary Lincoln explained in her 1886 book, *Mrs. Lincoln's Boston Cook Book: What to Do and What Not to Do in Cooking*, "Granulated sugar is brown sugar refined and re-crystallized. All brown and moist sugars are inferior in quality; they contain water and mineral matter. . . . [L]oaf sugar is the purest." This moisture is what gives brown sugar its tendency to clump and also to create baked goods that are softer, moister, and denser.

Sparkly Sugar Christmas Cookies

First extracted by ancient Egyptians, Greeks, and Romans by steeping rose petals in water, oil, or alcohol, rosewater spread to Europe via the Crusaders and was a popular flavoring in medieval England. It made its way to America with early colonists and shows up frequently in baked goods from the eighteenth and nineteenth centuries. It adds a delicate aroma and taste to these delightful cookies that "sparkle like frost-work," as described in the original recipe from Cookery and Domestic Economy *(1862).*

MAKES 3½ DOZEN COOKIES

1 stick (½ cup) unsalted butter, softened
1 cup sugar
1 teaspoon rosewater
¼ cup milk
2 cups all-purpose flour
1 teaspoon baking powder
½ teaspoon salt
White decorating sugar

Preheat oven to 350°F. Line baking sheets with parchment paper.

Using an electric mixer, cream the butter and sugar together in a bowl, then beat in the rosewater and milk.

Combine the flour, baking powder, and salt in a small bowl and add to the wet ingredients. Continue to mix until the ingredients form a soft dough.

Roll out the dough on a floured surface to a thickness of a little less than ¼ inch and cut into Christmas-themed shapes.

Place on baking sheets about 1 inch apart and sprinkle the cookie shapes with generous amounts of the white decorating sugar. Bake for 10–12 minutes. Cool for a few minutes on baking sheets and then transfer to wire racks to cool completely.

Very merry Christmas holiday postcard. NEW YORK PUBLIC LIBRARY DIGITAL COLLECTIONS

Christmas Stockings

It is generally believed that the custom of hanging up a Christmas stocking to receive presents stemmed from St. Nicholas's Day, celebrated on December 6 throughout medieval Europe. Folk traditions developed around the idea of St. Nicholas bringing treats to children on St. Nicholas's Eve (December 5). Children would leave their shoes by the fire that evening so St. Nicholas could slide down the chimney and fill them with treats such as fruit, nuts, and cookies. In some parts of Europe, stockings became a substitute for shoes.

Eventually, the tradition of giving gifts to children began to become associated with Christmas, prompted by the Protestant Reformation and the idea that the Christ Child (known as the Christkindel in Germany, sometimes depicted as a little girl in a white dress) was the gift giver, not St. Nicholas. As a result, German children began hanging stockings at the foot of their beds on Christmas Eve so the Christ Child could fill them with treats as she traveled from house to house. By the nineteenth century, this stocking custom had spread throughout Europe and had made its way to America, where Christkindel became "Kris Kringle."

By the Gilded Age, Christmas stockings were hung by the fireplace on Christmas Eve and filled with edible treats such as bonbons and other candy; cookies; small cakes; apples and oranges; and small gifts including items such as dolls, pencils, crayons, penknives, whistles, and telescopes. Larger gifts were often laid on chairs nearby. At first stockings were rather small (and indeed were typically actual plain black or white stockings), but they eventually grew in size, along with the magnitude and quantity of gifts, and became more colorful, with decorated stockings becoming more mainstream in the 1880s. As a result, sometimes a large stocking, several feet long, made especially for the purpose was hung up to receive all the presents. By the early twentieth century, gifts too large to fit in the stocking (such as ice skates, books, a doll's cradle, blocks, and puzzles) could be "deposited on the ground just below the stocking," according to a 1900 *Woman's Life* article.

Frosted Christmas Cookies

This original recipe, featured in an 1891 Independent *article "Some Christmas Dainties: For Old and Young" by Sara Sedgwick, was simply called "Christmas Cookies." According to Sedgwick, "Christmas cakes and cookies are very attractive to the little folks when baked in fanciful shapes and frosted with various colored icings," which she says to color a delicate pink, pale green, and light yellow. For the cookie shapes, she suggests using animal-themed cutters such as fish, dogs, cats, rabbits, and horses or botanical-shaped cutters such as leaves and flowers. Feel free to use store-bought food coloring for the icing or make your own based on Gilded Age–era recipes as shown below.*

MAKES ABOUT 4 DOZEN COOKIES

1½ sticks (¾ cup) unsalted butter, softened
1 cup sugar
1 egg
¼ cup milk
1 teaspoon lemon extract

4 cups all-purpose flour
1 teaspoon baking powder
½ teaspoon salt
⅓ cup dried currants

Preheat oven to 375°F. Line baking sheets with parchment paper.

Using an electric mixer, cream butter and sugar in a bowl until a pale yellow color. Beat in egg, then add milk and lemon extract. Mix until well combined.

In a separate bowl, combine flour with baking powder, salt, and currants. Stir well and add to the wet ingredients. Mix until currants are incorporated into the dough.

Roll out the dough on a floured surface to a thickness of a little more than ¼ inch and cut into cookie cutter shapes. Use a sharp knife to trim any stray currants around edges if needed.

Place about 2 inches apart on baking sheets. Bake for 10–12 minutes. Cool for a few minutes on baking sheets and then transfer to wire racks to cool completely.

When cool, decorate with colored frosting.

Colorants

Just as they are today, vibrantly hued confections were considered more appealing in the Gilded Age than those that were plain and colorless. But confectioners had to be careful—many of the substances used to color and brighten candies, icing, and other sweets were actually poisonous, such as arsenic, lead, copper, and zinc. Safe alternatives were often found using natural sources, including plants and spices such as saffron, turmeric, and marigold (to make yellow), spinach and raw coffee grains (to make green), and an insect called the cochineal (to make red or pink).

Cochineal is a bright red colorant made from the dried, pulverized bodies of the cochineal insect. Found in warmer locales such as Mexico, Central America, and the southwestern United States, these insects particularly enjoy feeding on cactus plants. Native Americans recognized the cochineal's dye-making properties long before the Europeans arrived in the New World, establishing plantations to harvest them in bulk. Europeans quickly caught on and were exporting cochineal overseas in the 1500s. (It is said that cochineal was used in the eighteenth century to dye the coats of the highest-ranking British officials a bright crimson color.) Chemists discovered that the carminic acid excreted by the insects could be mixed with aluminum or calcium salts to produce carmine, which was prized by confectioners as it produced an intense, brilliant scarlet color.

By the nineteenth century, cochineal powder was used not only by professional confectioners but also by home cooks who wanted to make their own decorating sugar and icings. Just a tiny bit could be used to make pink icing, and a few more drops would provide a deep red color. Icing could also be dyed a dark red by tinging it with tincture of saunders (a colorant made from the bark of the red sandalwood tree, native to India), which was also used to give gingerbread a red tint in medieval times. Other scarlet-hued coloring ingredients were the juice of ripe cherries, cranberries, or strawberries, which made "a very pretty icing for fruit cake . . . and also gave it a good flavor," according to *The Kentucky Housewife* (1837), by Lettice Bryan. Yellow icings, both deep and pale shades, were made with saffron juice or turmeric. Another method involved rubbing lumps of sugar against the rind of a "fine colored" lemon or orange, "which will at the same time flavor it sufficiently, without the aid of anything else," wrote Bryan. The juice of chopped spinach or other dark green vegetable was typically used to make green.

Frosted Christmas Cookies

CONTINUED

BASIC FROSTING

RECIPE (USING MODERN FOOD COLORING)

2 egg whites

4 cups sifted confectioners' sugar

2 teaspoons lemon juice

Place all the ingredients in a medium mixing bowl. Beat using an electric mixer on high speed until firm. Divide into three bowls and add a few drops of red food coloring to one, green to another, and yellow to the third, stirring after each addition to create the desired shades of pale pink, green, and yellow icing.

ICING MADE WITH NATURAL COLORANTS

PINK FROSTING

1 egg white

2 cups sifted confectioners' sugar

1 teaspoon tart cherry or cranberry juice

Place all the ingredients in a medium mixing bowl. Beat using an electric mixer on high speed until spreadable consistency. Add a few more drops of juice to obtain the desired color and consistency if needed.

Frosted Christmas Cookies

YELLOW FROSTING

1 egg white

2 cups sifted confectioners' sugar

1 teaspoon lemon juice

½–1 teaspoon turmeric

Place egg white, sugar, and lemon juice in a medium mixing bowl. Beat using an electric mixer on high speed until firm. Add ½ teaspoon turmeric, mixing well to combine, and then add additional amounts ¼ teaspoon at a time to obtain desired color. Add a few more drops of lemon juice to obtain spreadable consistency.

PALE GREEN FROSTING

2 cups packed washed fresh spinach leaves (stems removed)

1 cup water

1 egg white

2 cups sifted confectioners' sugar

To make spinach juice, add spinach and water to a small saucepan. Bring to a boil, then turn heat to medium and cook for 15 minutes. When done, set aside and allow to steep and cool (about 15 minutes). When cool, drain liquid through a fine sieve over a small measuring cup. Set liquid aside. (Alternately, you can also use bottled spinach or kale juice instead of cooking down fresh spinach and skip this step.)

Place egg white, sugar, and 1 teaspoon spinach juice in a medium mixing bowl. Beat using an electric mixer on high speed until firm. Add a few more drops of spinach juice to obtain color and consistency if needed.

Barnum's Animal Crackers: A Christmas Marketing Opportunity

The art of crafting baked goods into fancy shapes and molds (including animals) was often associated with Christmas in medieval Germany, and these intricate cookies were frequently used as holiday decorations. The idea caught on and spread through Europe, and by the mid-1800s small cookies (known as biscuits in the United Kingdom) baked into fancy shapes were a popular treat in Victorian England, often mass manufactured in new factories. Many of these were designed in the shape of animals (and were, in fact, called Animals). When showman P. T. Barnum decided to tour England with his circus in 1889, several companies got caught up in this marketing opportunity and began making circus-animal-themed biscuits.

The concept quickly made its way over to America and was adopted by various companies, including Hetfield & Ducker in Brooklyn and Vandeveer & Holmes Biscuit Company in New York. These two companies, along with other baking manufacturers, were merged to form the New York Biscuit Company (later named Nabisco), which changed the popular product's name to Barnum's Animal Crackers in 1902 (although Barnum apparently never received a cent for lending his name, according to a 2001 *Washington Post* article). It was an ingenious and novel marketing idea, introducing Gilded Age folks to a new type of animal cracker, sold in a small, festively colored red-and-green box resembling a circus train with a string at the top so it could be used as a Christmas tree ornament. But what was originally introduced as a holiday season novelty became a popular, steady seller that is still sold in a little box with a string. Since then there have been at least fifty-three different animal cracker shapes, ranging from lions, tigers, and bears (oh my!) to monkeys, hyenas, and koalas.

Sand Tarts

Also called sand cookies, these crispy sugar cookies were a popular Gilded Age holiday treat. The inspiration for the name originated from the egg glaze and sprinkling of coarse cinnamon sugar on top of each cookie, giving them a sandy appearance. Some nineteenth-century recipes also called for a topping of chopped, halved, or whole almonds or hickory nuts, or a single raisin.

MAKES 3 DOZEN COOKIES

2 eggs
1 cup sugar
½ stick (4 tablespoons) salted butter, softened
2¼ cups flour
3 tablespoons white decorating sugar
½ teaspoon cinnamon
Additional granulated sugar
1 egg white, beaten

Preheat oven to 375°F. Line baking sheets with parchment paper.

Using an electric mixer, beat eggs and sugar in a bowl until fluffy. Add butter and continue to beat until well mixed.

Add flour and continue to mix until a stiff dough forms (may need to add ¼ cup more if dough seems sticky).

Combine decorating sugar and cinnamon in a small bowl and set aside.

Sprinkle a thick coating of granulated sugar on a clean counter or pastry board. Roll out dough on this surface very thin (about ⅛ inch) and cut into desired shapes. Transfer to baking sheets and place about 1 inch apart. Brush lightly with beaten egg white, then sprinkle with some of the cinnamon and sugar mixture.

Bake for 8–10 minutes until crisp around the edges. Transfer from baking sheets to wire rack to cool completely.

Brown Sugar Cookies

Gilded Age–era cookbooks are chock-full of brown sugar cookie recipes. The version below takes bits and pieces of recipes from The Home Queen World's Fair Souvenir Cook Book *(1893),* Berea Cook Book *(1897), and* The A.A. Cook Book: Containing Three Hundred Tested Recipes *(1895). The larger-grained Demerara sugar is similar to what was used at the time and creates a cookie that is chewy and soft in the middle with a delightful crunch and slight toffee flavor.*

MAKES 3 DOZEN COOKIES

- 1 stick (½ cup) unsalted butter, softened
- 1 cup Demerara sugar
- 2 eggs
- 2¼ cups all-purpose flour
- 1 teaspoon baking soda
- 1 teaspoon ginger
- ½ teaspoon salt
- Additional Demerara sugar

Preheat oven to 400°F. Line baking sheets with parchment paper.

Using an electric mixer, cream butter and sugar in a bowl on medium-high speed until well blended. Mix in the eggs.

Sift together flour, baking soda, ginger, and salt in a separate bowl. Add to wet ingredients and mix until well combined.

Scoop dough into walnut-sized balls and roll in Demerara sugar. Add flour in small increments if dough seems sticky.

Place 2 inches apart on baking sheets and bake for 8–10 minutes. Let stand for a minute or two, then transfer cookies to a wire rack to cool completely.

Holiday Jumbles

Rich with generous amounts of butter, egg, and sugar, jumbles are one of the first cookie types popularized in America and were a common fixture in nineteenth-century American cookbooks. The dough was typically seasoned with spices such as freshly grated nutmeg, cinnamon, and mace, as well as rosewater or lemon essence, which added a delicate layer of flavor. Named for the Latin word gemel, *which means "twin," jumbles were originally shaped like a figure eight or double ring. To make preparation quicker and easier, it became customary for Americans to form the dough into single rings. By the late nineteenth century, many cooks rolled out the dough, cut it into rounds, and then stamped out the middles. Once cool, they can be decorated with green-tinted frosting to resemble a holiday wreath.*

2 sticks (1 cup) unsalted butter, softened
1 cup sugar
1 egg
1 tablespoon rosewater (or lemon essence)

3 cups sifted flour
2 teaspoons freshly grated nutmeg
½ teaspoon mace
½ teaspoon cinnamon
Additional granulated sugar

Preheat the oven to 375°F. Line baking sheets with parchment paper.

Using an electric mixer, cream butter and sugar until a very pale yellow color. Add egg and rosewater, blending thoroughly.

Sift flour with spices in a separate bowl. Add all at once to the creamed mixture, blending well. Wrap the dough in plastic wrap and chill for at least 2 hours.

On a lightly floured surface, roll out the dough to ⅛ inch thickness. Cut out shapes with a plain round cookie cutter or one that is round and scalloped around the edges (like a flower). Use a small bottle cap or thimble to hollow out the center of each circle.

Place cookies about 1 inch apart on baking sheets and bake for 10–12 minutes or until lightly browned around the edges. Remove from baking sheets to wire rack and allow to cool. Once cool, decorate as follows:

HOLIDAY JUMBLES

CONTINUED

FROSTING

2 cups confectioners' sugar

2 tablespoons water

Green food coloring

Sift confectioners' sugar into a shallow bowl. Add water and stir together until smooth and well blended. Add enough green food coloring to yield an evergreen shade. You can add a little lemon juice or more water if it seems too stiff. Spread a little on each cookie and then sprinkle on red, green, and/or white cookie decorations. If you want to get more fancy, spoon icing into a pastry bag (you may need to thin it a little more with water) and pipe frosting around each cookie to simulate wreath greens. You can also tint a little bit of icing red and pipe a bow on each wreath.

A Currier and Ives Christmas

When Nathanial Currier started a print shop in Lower Manhattan in the early 1830s, he was a trailblazer in the new field of lithography, an innovative method of creating complicated black-and-white images using a grease crayon to draw an image on a porous surface. When mounted in a press, the surface worked as a printing block to produce clear, concise images. Like many Gilded Age inventions, it was a time saver. At first his focus was on current events, such as the deadly fire on the American steamship *Lexington*; his print appeared in the *New York Sun* and helped launch his career. Soon he hired a slew of illustrators and was able to mass-produce an average of three to four unlimited-edition new prints per week. In the 1850s he partnered with James Ives, who helped streamline the business operations. Eventually the print house expanded its repertoire, focusing on the Civil War, sporting events, historic Americana, and of course wintry scenes such as snowy landscapes, farmhouses, and sleigh rides, which aligned perfectly with the Christmas season. Indeed, even today Currier & Ives is often synonymous with Christmas cards.

Christmas Cards

Christmas cards are said to have originated in England in the 1840s from a design created by John Alcott Horsley, a painter and illustrator for Sir Henry Cole, the first director of London's Victoria and Albert Museum. The card depicted a festive family scene and the greeting, "A Merry Christmas and a Happy New Year to You." According to a *Washington Post* article, the original purpose of the Christmas card was both practical and sentimental, enabling its sender to "side-step the expense of a gift and at the same time hold a franchise on friendship." By midcentury the concept had become more popular, and by the Gilded Age Christmas cards were regularly exchanged, with fancy and frilly designs similar to Valentine's Day cards. This was likely due to the fact that firms already producing valentines also started to print Christmas cards, sometimes with the same lacy borders, floral sprays, and cherub images. But soon more Christmassy themed cards began to take hold, with pictures depicting bells, snowy landscapes, Yule logs, and holly and ivy becoming mainstream.

In the United States, a gentleman named Louis Prang pushed the needle for Christmas cards. Prang was a German printing entrepreneur who arrived in New England in 1850 and expanded his business (including the lithographic techniques also used by Currier & Ives) over the next twenty-five years, launching Christmas greeting cards in 1875. By the 1880s he had three hundred employees printing more than five million holiday cards each year. Around this time, Prang also had the savvy idea to host a contest for Christmas card designs. It was held at the American Art Gallery on East 23rd Street in New York City, and L. Prang & Co. offered $2,000 for first, second, third, and fourth prizes depicting "the best original design for a Christmas card painted in watercolor or oil." Judges for this Prang Prize Competition included the proprietors of the American Art Gallery, John La Farge, Samuel Colman, and Louis C. Tiffany, the famous artist/decorator who created the Tiffany lamp and other stained glass and decorative work.

The Yule Log

The yule log has its origins more in pagan customs than in the Nativity story. During winter solstice a large log was burned at a solemn gathering, where it was blessed and a piece set aside to start the bonfire the following year. One legend says that Norsemen burned oak logs in honor of the god Thor, and another that Celtic folks believed perpetual fire was sacred, continuing the tradition of using a piece of the prior year's log.

Eventually in England the custom evolved into a festive ceremony during which all household members (men, women, and children) traveled into the woods to select a huge log (typically of ash, hickory, or oak) to burn on Christmas Eve through Christmas Day. It was often first decorated with branches of mistletoe and other greenery and then tied up with a strong rope so it could be dragged home through the snow, while the celebrants sang Christmas carols. Children were often allowed to ride on top of the log as it was brought inside. In large houses with sizable fireplaces, the log was sometimes permitted to smolder until Twelfth Night (January 6).

The yule log concept spread throughout Europe, where the French even devised a cake (called a *bûche de noël)* in the shape of a yule log, iced with chocolate frosting to simulate bark. In America the yule log went through even more changes, including the idea of a diminutive version made from birch wood. A 1909 *Harper's Bazaar* magazine suggests fastening holly branches with a bit of wire around and on top of the yule log to look as if the holly is growing out of the log. This article described this charming holiday decoration as suitable for "a dainty table."

BUTTER COOKIES

Butter was traditionally a luxury item because it was expensive and would turn bad easily. Like sugar, it was a highly prized ingredient for baked goods such as cakes, pies, pastries, and cookies. Before the Gilded Age (before refrigeration became more available), butter was preserved with salt. But just as today, cooks and bakers preferred using unsalted (fresh) butter to make the finest cakes and cookies, so they actually "washed" their butter before using it, kneading it in cool water to release some of the salt. Some recipes even called for washing the butter in rosewater, perhaps to impart some of this delicate taste to the baked goods.

In America's early days, most butter was made on rural farms and then sold at nearby city markets. By the early 1860s, this dairy commodity became more widely accessible when butter factories (or "creameries") began to produce butter in larger quantities. The first creameries were launched in upstate New York, led by Alanson Slaughter, who employed a concept that had been used by cheesemakers: the collective pooling of milk by dairy farmers.

But it was a Gilded Age invention, the mechanical cream separator, that truly industrialized butter production. Creameries previously had to wait for cream to rise to the top of separating vats. This innovation used the concept of centrifugal force to separate the heavier butterfat particles from the lighter, watery milk portions, allowing cream to be separated from whole milk in a matter of minutes rather than days. This not only expedited the process but also significantly decreased the cost.

Around the same time, advances in food science allowed for commercial production of unsalted butter. Factory production of butter went from 29 million pounds in 1879, to 627 million in 1909, to over 1 billion in 1921. In the nineteenth century, butter was marketed mainly in tubs and portioned out by the grocer to individual buyers, but by late in the century packaged butter came into play, with the Beatrice Creamery Company being the first to market it in 1898.

As a result, many more cookie varieties could be made all over the country, especially at Christmas. Here are a few Gilded Age favorites.

Scotch Shortbread

Shortbread dates back to the twelfth century, originating in Great Britain as a "biscuit bread" made from leftover bread dough. Eventually butter was used as the shortening, which made it quite a luxury item since butter was expensive. It is the large amount of butter that makes these cookies crumbly like a short crust pastry. The other core ingredients are flour and sugar, although flavorings such as caraway, lemon, and almond have also been added over the years. During the Gilded Age, shortbread was often sent as a gift to friends at Christmas time, typically baked in a large round pie shape. White sugar icing was used to write the name of the recipient in the center and decorate the edges. This recipe came to my family via my Aunt Joan Mansell and is always a favorite at Christmas!

MAKES 8–10 WEDGES

2 sticks (1 cup) unsalted butter
2 cups flour
1 cup cornstarch
1 cup confectioners' sugar
Granulated sugar (for sprinkling on top)

Preheat oven to 325°F.

Melt butter in a saucepan over low heat. Remove from heat and stir in flour, cornstarch, and confectioners' sugar. Mix well (may need to use hands to mix, as the dough can be crumbly).

Place dough in an ungreased 8-inch pie plate, pressing down to cover the bottom of the pan. Prick all over with a table fork. Bake for 25–30 minutes (edges can brown, so check after 25 minutes). Sprinkle with granulated sugar and cut into wedges immediately. Place pie plate on a wire rack to cool.

If planning to give the shortbread as a gift, I suggest using an 8-inch round disposable aluminum pan. Prick all over with a table fork and bake for 25–30 minutes. Place on a wire rack to cool. When cool, decorate using the icing and instructions below.

Mary
John

Scotch Shortbread

CONTINUED

ICING

1 egg white

2 cups sifted confectioners' sugar

1 teaspoon lemon juice

Place all ingredients in a medium mixing bowl. Beat using an electric mixer on high speed until firm. The icing should be of a thin enough consistency to flow through a fine pastry tube. Add a few more drops of lemon juice or water to obtain this consistency if needed. To decorate the shortbread, write the name of the recipient in the center and embellish the edges as desired.

Merry Christmas holiday postcard: sprigs of mistletoe and holly. NEW YORK PUBLIC LIBRARY DIGITAL COLLECTIONS

Christmas Wrapping

For those women who were not part of the Gilded Age well-to-do set, homemade gifts of baked goods were popular, often given in packages that were both pretty and practical. Many ladies would be on the lookout throughout the year for containers that could be used for Christmas gift giving. For example, jars of jelly or jam were repurposed by painting them red or green and stenciling them with holly leaves and red berries. Small boxes were covered with green crepe paper and lined with white tissue to hold cookies, macaroons, candies, and small cakes, then tied with crimson ribbon and a bunch of holly.

An article from a December 1902 issue of *Collier's Once a Week* magazine suggested food gifts such as a plum pudding steamed in an attractive mold, covered in waxed paper, then wrapped in moss green tissue paper, tied with a bright red satin ribbon, and topped with a festive sprig of holly. Another idea was to make a batch of fresh doughnuts, sprinkle them with liberal amounts of confectioners' sugar, and nestle them inside a dark green wicker basket lined with snowy-white tissue paper. A scarlet satin ribbon and holly branch tied on the handle of the basket added a festive touch of color.

A December 1888 *Good Housekeeping* article titled "Baskets for Christmas" recommended giving gift baskets filled with enjoyable treats such as flowers, fruit, sweetmeats, or "better still, some trifle of cookery made by the giver's own hands." These were particularly special if given to "a friend who is entirely able to gratify all desires and fancies, but will appreciate our handiwork in any form," and at the other end of the spectrum, "the sensitive individual who can make no present in return, but who will be pleased and touched with a little gift of greeting." Plain wicker baskets were painted gold, silver, or copper and lined with a paper napkin, then filled with cakes or candies. A vibrant bow added a contrast of color to the handle, such as scarlet with gold, light blue with silver and peacock blue, or yellow with copper.

Other edible gift offerings included mince or pumpkin pies, ramekins of salted peanuts or almonds, brandied cherries dipped in fondant and set inside individual miniature paper cases, attractively packaged cheese straws, and boxes of stuffed dates or pralines. Popcorn was a favorite food gift for the younger set, and quarts of fresh, liberally buttered popcorn were often presented in wooden pails, especially for those households that had several children. Popcorn balls were another gift idea, often packaged up in twists of tissue paper along with a few cookies. "Then you are prepared for the boys and girls, little and big; even the old folks won't despise them," claimed an article from an 1882 issue of *Ohio Farmer*.

German Butter Cookies

Cardamom has been associated with Christmas baking in Germany since the Middle Ages. The dried fruit of the perennial herb Elettaria cardamomum, *cardamom is the third most expensive spice, after saffron and vanilla. In Scandinavia and Germany, it is used extensively as a flavoring in baked goods, as well as pickles.*

MAKES 4½ DOZEN COOKIES

FOR THE COOKIES

2 sticks (1 cup) unsalted butter, softened

1 cup sugar

1 egg

1 tablespoon milk

3 cups all-purpose flour

1 teaspoon cardamom

½ teaspoon salt

FOR THE TOPPING

1 egg, beaten

½ cup sugar

¼ cup finely chopped almonds

½ teaspoon cinnamon

Preheat oven to 375°F. Line baking sheets with parchment paper.

To make the cookies, using an electric mixer, cream the butter and sugar together in a bowl, then beat in the egg and milk.

Sift the flour with the cardamom and salt in a separate bowl, then slowly add to the wet ingredients.

Roll out the dough on a floured surface to a thickness of a little less than ¼ inch and cut into shapes using Christmas cookie cutters. Place 1 inch apart on baking sheets.

To make the topping, break the egg into a small dish and beat lightly. In a separate bowl, mix together the sugar, almonds, and cinnamon. Lightly brush each cookie with the beaten egg and then sprinkle with the sugar-almond-cinnamon mixture.

Bake for 10 minutes or until lightly browned. Cool for a few minutes and then transfer from the baking sheets to wire racks and let cool completely.

GALETTES

These delightful little cakes are buttery and not too sweet, similar to a tea cake or a scone. To jazz them up, feel free to add ½ cup raisins or dried currants to the dough with the flour. According to Mrs. Hale's New Cook Book *(1857), by Sarah Josepha Hale, these cakes were favorites in France and could be made "rich, and comparatively delicate" for special occasions or "quite common," depending on the amount of butter and size of the cookie cutter used. Sarah Tyson Rorer included these treats in a 1906* Ladies Home Journal *article titled "Some Good Christmas Cookies." They are a perfect addition to a holiday tea table.*

 MAKES ABOUT 1 DOZEN SMALL CAKES 

FOR THE CAKES

1 stick (½ cup) unsalted butter, softened

⅔ cup sugar

2 egg yolks

¼ cup milk

½ teaspoon salt

2¾ cups all-purpose flour

FOR THE GLAZED TOPPING

1 egg, beaten

1 tablespoon sugar

1 tablespoon milk

Preheat oven to 350°F. Line baking sheets with parchment paper.

To make the cakes, beat the butter and sugar in a large bowl until creamy. Slowly add the egg yolks and milk, alternating between the two, until well blended.

Add the salt and flour in small increments until a smooth paste forms. (Dough will be slightly sticky.) Flatten dough into a disk shape and cover with plastic wrap. Chill in the refrigerator for at least 1 hour.

Roll out dough on a floured surface to a thickness of ½–¾ inch. Cut into shapes with a round or fluted 3-inch cookie cutter and place 1 inch apart on baking sheet. Prick all over with a fork.

Make the glaze by combining the beaten egg, sugar, and milk in a small dish. Lightly brush this mixture on top of each small cake. (You will not use all of it; feel free to reserve the rest to make French toast.)

Bake for 15–17 minutes until the cakes are still slightly soft to the touch. Cool for a few minutes on the baking sheet and then transfer to a wire rack and let cool completely.

Christmas Tea Parties

The holiday season was a popular occasion for tea parties, particularly in large cities such as New York, Philadelphia, Pittsburgh, and Washington, D.C. Many of these were yearly events, such as the one given by Joseph and Martha Albree of Pittsburgh. Joseph was a partner in the George Albree, Son and Company shoe store (named after Joseph's father George, who was the founder), then later went into the ornamental iron work business with his sons. According to a December 1897 article from the *Pittsburg Post*, Martha's cheerful hospitality made these annual affairs "among the pleasantest occasions of the season," and the tea that year was an "especially brilliant event." The Albrees' son Frederick and his new bride were the guests of honor at the tea, which was held in the "handsome old home" where

LYNDHURST MANSION, TARRYTOWN, NY

the Albree family had resided for several generations. It was lavishly decorated with holly and flowers, with the drawing room decked out in pink-and-white hyacinths, carnations, and roses. The dining room where the tea took place featured a large poinsettia centerpiece and crimson shaded candles.

Other yearly teas were affiliated with clubs or groups, such as the Washington Wellesley Club (founded in 1888 as the first Wellesley College Alumnae Club). According to an article in the *Washington Post*, the club's annual Christmas tea in 1902 was hosted by Dr. Louise Tayler Jones (who later became president of the American Medical Women's Association) at her home on 21st and O Streets. Refreshments were served, and college girls home for the holiday break "renewed the youth of the others with their bright tales of present-day Wellesley." And the South End Wheelmen of Philadelphia (a bicycling club) held an annual Christmas tea at their clubhouse on South Broad Street, where gifts were given to members, including items such as mirrors, vases, and bicycle grips.

Some teas were held as charitable events, such as the Christmas tea given to students at St. Peter's Industrial School in Philadelphia in 1901 by Mrs. Eleanor Widener. Several other women from prominent social and church circles assisted Mrs. Widener with the tea, which included a short religious service and ended with everyone singing Christmas carols.

Eleanor was the wife of streetcar magnate George D. Widener from Elkins Park, Pennsylvania, heir to one of the largest fortunes in Philadelphia at the time. A decade later, the Wideners were tragically on board the RMS *Titanic* in 1912, along with their oldest son Harry, and while Eleanor and her maid were able to get on board one of the lifeboats and were later rescued, George and Harry perished in the disaster.

Debutante Parties

Afternoon teas that doubled as debutante or coming out parties (events at which young ladies made their debut into society) were also fashionable. These were typically larger events, more akin to a ball, such as the Christmas tea given in 1893 by Fannie Morris Clarke (wife of Thomas Benedict Clarke, an art collector/dealer and adviser to J. P. Morgan) at their home on West 44th Street in New York City. The event featured an afternoon tea for six hundred people, including ladies from famous families such as the Rockefellers, Schuylers, Parkers, and Posts. This large reception was followed by a more intimate dinner for eighteen people at 7:30 p.m. (at which Mrs. Clarke could put more focus on introducing her daughter to her preferred suitors), and then a dance. Later in the evening, the entire party went to the Vaudeville Club performance at the Metropolitan Opera House. So, quite a lengthy night!

Debutante dances were also a common occurrence during Christmas week, particularly in large cities such as New York, Philadelphia, and Washington, D.C. This was likely because potential suitors were home from college during the holiday break. Some of these events were given in private homes, while others were held in restaurants such as New York's Delmonico's and Rauscher's in Washington, D.C. Rauscher's was a famous fine dining establishment run by Charles Rauscher, a French confectioner and caterer who had trained under world-class chefs in Paris and came to America during the height of the Gilded Age. For many years he worked as steward at Sherry's in New York, before going to Washington to open his own restaurant and catering business at Connecticut Avenue and L Street. He became well connected with government officials and served as the caterer for inaugural balls, White House weddings, and hundreds of prominent Washington-area social events.

Apricot Tea Cookies

Aprikosen Gebäck

Apricots grow abundantly in the Black Forest, where Germans enjoy them fresh, dried, in baked goods, and preserved. This recipe calls for combining two flavorful preparations: buttery coconut almond cookies and sweet apricot preserves. These cookies present a harmony of flavors and are delicious with coffee or tea or, arranged in pretty tins, make for sweet holiday gifts.

5 cups all-purpose flour, sifted
2 teaspoons baking powder
½ teaspoon salt
4 sticks (1 pound) unsalted butter, softened
¾ cup granulated sugar
2 large eggs
1 cup sliced almonds, toasted
1 cup apricot preserves
¼ cup flaked coconut, toasted

Line baking sheets with parchment paper.

Sift together the flour, baking powder, and salt in a medium bowl.

Place the butter in the bowl of an electric stand mixer fitted with the paddle attachment and begin mixing on medium speed. While mixing, add the sugar in a steady stream and continue mixing until light and fluffy, stopping at least once to scrape down the sides of the bowl. Add the eggs one at a time and continue to mix until incorporated, again stopping at least once to scrape down the sides of the bowl.

Reduce the mixing speed to low and gradually incorporate the sifted dry ingredients, mixing until just combined. Add the almonds, ½ cup of the preserves, and the coconut, mixing until incorporated. Wrap the dough in plastic wrap and chill in the refrigerator for at least 1 hour.

Preheat the oven to 350°F.

Apricot Tea Cookies

CONTINUED

Shape the dough into 1-inch balls and place 1 inch apart on the prepared baking sheets. Make an indentation (using your thumb is best) in the center of each ball and fill with about ½ teaspoon of the remaining preserves. Bake until the edges of the cookies are lightly browned, about 12–15 minutes. Transfer the cookies from the baking sheets to wire racks and let cool completely. Store in an airtight container.

Excerpted from Walter Staib, Black Forest Cuisine *(Philadelphia: Running Press, 2006)*

Fruit Trees and Christmas

The tradition of bringing holly, ivy, and evergreens into the home is said to go back to Roman times. Presenting evergreens (thought to be a token of good luck) to others was common during winter celebrations in ancient Rome. This idea carried over into the sixth century in the area where present-day Germany is, where residents adorned houses with laurel and tree boughs, believing that decorating their homes with greenery would give them good luck for the year. The tradition of the Christmas tree emerged several centuries later, soon migrating to England and then the rest of the world. By the early 1800s, in addition to a fir Christmas tree, many Germans placed a huge pot containing a cherry or apricot tree in the corner of the room, starting in November so that it was in full bloom by Christmas. It was a prized ornament that added much to the festive joy of the Christmas season and provided a bit of friendly competition as families vied with each other to have the finest fruit tree.

This custom carried over to America, enjoyed by the Pennsylvania Dutch in the form of tabletop branches of cherry trees or a large limb from an evergreen shrub, such as mountain laurel or cedar. These tabletop trees, laden with huge assortments of sweet ornaments, were displayed in large flowerpots and surrounded with plates of festive food. Common ornaments included jumbles (page 31), gingerbread cookies (page 13), marzipan cherries, and small baskets of candy. The concept was also adopted by many churches in the 1840s and 1850s as a means of teaching children about Christian values. These trees quickly became a Gilded Age status symbol.

LYNDHURST MANSION, TARRYTOWN, NY

CAKES

Many rich cakes improve with age, and it has always been the custom with the best Southern housekeepers to make their Christmas cakes several weeks in advance of the holidays.

—ELIZA R. PARKER, *HARPER'S BAZAAR*, 1892

Whipped Cream Cakes
Spice Gems
Lemon Gingerbread
Dominoes
Christmas Cake
Fudgy Chocolate Cake

AT THE START of the Gilded Age, many seasonal cakes were of the fruitcake variety, rich and heavy and containing lots of dried fruit, spices, and nuts. But by the latter part of the nineteenth century, lighter flour-based cake varieties also became popular to serve during the holidays. One reason for this is likely the proliferation of labor-saving devices that made baking these types of cakes much easier.

One of these important kitchen conveniences was the rotary eggbeater, first patented in 1863, with other patents following in rapid succession. In the 1870s the Dover Stamping Company of Boston emerged as the best known manufacturer of the device. Dover's original patent involved a side-mounted gear wheel that rotated wire wings to beat the eggs more efficiently. Called the Dover, it came in a wide range of sizes appropriate for individuals, families, and hotels. By the 1880s there were many different types of eggbeaters on the market, with new design tweaks launched constantly, such as a design featuring a wire whip or French eggbeater, a wire spoon, a spiral eggbeater, and a variety of rotary models. All of these would have been a revelation to cooks who had previously had to beat eggs by hand, a tedious and tiring process that could take an hour or more and was often delegated to a servant. Timing as well as the equipment used were important; if the eggs were not beaten correctly (especially the yolks), the cake could end up heavy, tough, and streaky, with an "eggy" taste.

Another life-changing nineteenth-century invention was the adoption of leavening agents, such as pearlash (potassium carbonate, refined potash obtained from wood ashes), saleratus (an early form of baking soda), and baking soda. When baking powder came on the scene in the late 1850s, quick breads became popular, and sky-high layer cakes could be produced with much less effort. Recipes for baked goods that formerly called for eggs and yeast to make them rise replaced these traditional ingredients with this new time-saving substance. A new era in baking was born, and many recipes were restructured to incorporate the substitute. Even though cookbook writers like Eliza Leslie warned, "If too much is used, they will impart a disagreeable taste," ease won out over the chance of any chemical flavors. Many cooks would compromise a little on natural freshness for the assistance and time savings these newfangled additives provided, especially when a recipe such as for milk biscuits called for kneading the mixture for forty minutes. In addition, these new leavenings improved over time, producing light and airy cakes of all types in a fraction of the time.

By the early 1900s, holiday cakes became more ingenious and decorative. For example, Christmas shortcake was made from sponge cake rounds generously spread with whipped cream and topped with stars of bright red jelly (gelatin). Another interesting dessert was a banana crown with snowball cakes, made by carefully removing the fruit portion of bananas and then filling the peels with ice cream. They were then arranged in a circle on a platter, and balls of cake that had been rolled in icing and grated coconut were placed in the center to resemble snowballs.

Place Cards at Christmas Dinner

Photography was a novel nineteenth-century technology that was continually undergoing refinements throughout the Gilded Age. A 1902 *Boston Cooking School Magazine* article contains directions on how to make Christmas place cards out of blueprints (also known as cyanotype photography). Invented by William Herschel (the son of astronomer Sir William Herschel) in 1842, cyanotype is still in use today. Originally intended for reproducing math tables, the process involves laying an object on paper coated with iron salts, then exposing it to ultraviolet light and rinsing it with water to create brilliant blue-and-white images. In this case, a photograph of each person would be used to make the blueprint to serve as a place card. Instead of using names, the hostess would write each guest's favorite expression underneath their image, and a treasure hunt for everyone's assigned spots would follow. As stated in the article, "Let all find their places, and much fun will ensue. . . . In every family group some pet hobby or familiar expression can be used to arouse merriment and make a novel place-card—a souvenir, perhaps, to hang in one's room until next Christmas."

Whipped Cream Cakes

Gilded Age cookbooks are chock-full of recipes for small cakes (what we call cupcakes today) that feature any number of tasty fillings. In addition to whipped cream cakes, cream cakes were another era favorite, made by hollowing out cupcakes and filling them with vanilla custard pudding. Jelly was another popular filling ingredient, such as in a recipe for fancy cakes in the cookbook Culinary Gems: A Collection of Choice Recipes Gathered with Care from the Treasures of Culinary Experts *(1884). The light and fluffy cakes featured here pair wonderfully with the rich whipped cream topping. Adding a cherry or strawberry as a garnish adds a festive touch.*

FOR THE CUPCAKES

1 stick (½ cup) salted butter, softened

1 cup sugar

2 eggs

1 teaspoon vanilla

2 cups cake flour

2 teaspoons baking powder

¾ cup whole milk

FOR THE WHIPPED CREAM

2 cups (1 pint) heavy cream

4 tablespoons confectioners' sugar

2 teaspoons vanilla

Fresh strawberries or cherries (for garnish)

Preheat oven to 350°F.

Line 18 cupcake or muffin tins with cupcake liners. Place a steel mixing bowl and beater(s) in the freezer (for making whipped cream later).

Using an electric mixer on a medium-high speed, cream the butter and sugar in a bowl until fluffy. Turn down to medium and beat in the eggs one at a time, then add the vanilla.

In a separate bowl, sift the flour and baking powder together. With the mixer set to a low speed, add to the wet ingredients, alternating with the milk. Mix until just combined.

Using a spoon or scoop, drop batter into lined cupcake tins. They should be about two-thirds full. Place on the bottom two racks of the oven and bake for 20 minutes

Whipped Cream Cakes

or until a toothpick inserted into the center comes out clean. Remove from the tins and let cool on wire rack.

While the cakes are cooling, make the whipped cream. Remove the mixing bowl and beater(s) from the freezer. Add the heavy cream, confectioners' sugar, and vanilla to the bowl and whip using an electric mixer on medium speed for about 5 minutes or until firm peaks form. Leave bowl in the refrigerator until cakes are cool.

When cakes are completely cool, take a sharp knife and hollow out a small circle in the top of each cupcake. Place about a tablespoon of whipped cream inside the hollow space and replace the top. Frost all over with the remaining whipped cream. Garnish with a strawberry slice or cherry.

Christmas Dishware

The Gilded Age was also the period when the first decorative Christmas plate was introduced, launched by Danish company Bing & Grondahl in 1895. Called "Behind the Frosted Window," these seven-inch, blue-and-white porcelain plates featured a bas relief design hand painted in shades of what became known as "Copenhagen blue" using an underglaze technique. They cost about 50 cents apiece at the time. They were so successful that the company released "New Moon over Snow Covered Trees" the following year, and "Christmas Meal of the Sparrows" in 1897. Today all of these plates are highly regarded by collectors and can fetch prices in the thousands of dollars.

Other Scandinavian companies soon followed suit, with Swedish pottery company Rorstrand launching its first Christmas plate series in 1904, and Royal Copenhagen (also from Denmark) issuing its first Christmas pattern, "Madonna and Child," in 1908. This was hand painted in the same shade of blue and same underglaze technique of bas belief on porcelain as Bing & Grondahl's. The main difference was that it featured a wider border, and by this time the cost was upward of $1 per plate. Norwegian pottery firm Porsgrund released its first Christmas plate in 1909. The Spode "Christmas Tree" dishware pattern that graces many holiday dinner and dessert tables today was not issued until 1938.

Spice Gems

Gems are little muffin-like cakes that were extremely popular in the nineteenth and early twentieth centuries. The key to baking them was to place the batter in a hot, well-buttered gem pan. Patented by Nathaniel Waterman of Boston in 1859, gem pans were shallower than today's muffin pans and made of cast iron, which caused the gem to puff up nicely, particularly when the pan was heated in the oven ahead of time. As instructed by Dr. Chase's Third, Last and Complete Receipt Book *(1895), "the gem pans being warm, or hot, and buttered, dip in the batter to half fill them, for, if properly prepared, they will raise to fill the pans."*

 **MAKES 8 GEMS OR 1 DOZEN CUPCAKES** 

2 ounces unsweetened baking chocolate
2 tablespoons unsalted butter, softened
1 cup sugar
2 eggs
1½ cups all-purpose flour
1½ teaspoons baking powder
¼ teaspoon salt
1 teaspoon cinnamon
1 teaspoon ginger
⅛ teaspoon cloves
⅓ cup milk
Vegetable oil or melted butter for greasing the pan

Place a cast-iron gem pan in the oven on the middle rack and preheat oven to 375°F. Alternatively, line a 12-cup muffin pan with cupcake papers and preheat oven to 375°F.

Place the chocolate in a microwave-safe dish and heat in the microwave on high for 30 seconds. Take out the dish and give the chocolate a stir. Continue doing this in 30-second intervals until chocolate is melted. Set aside.

Cream butter and sugar in a bowl until a pale yellow color, then add eggs. Mix well, then add melted chocolate.

In a separate bowl, sift together flour, baking powder, salt, and spices. Add to wet ingredients either using the low speed of an electric mixer or stirring by hand, alternating with the milk until just incorporated.

Spice Gems

CONTINUED

Carefully remove gem pan from oven. Using a pastry brush, grease the pan cups with a generous amount of oil or melted butter. Spoon batter into each cup so that it is two-thirds full. If using a regular muffin pan, spoon batter into each cup so that it is one-half to two-thirds full.

Return pan to the middle rack of the oven and bake for 15–18 minutes, or until toothpick inserted in the center comes out clean. Cool in pan on wire rack for about 20 minutes, then remove from pan by running a knife around the edge of each gem cup and lifting out with a small spatula. Let cool completely, then frost with maple butter frosting.

MAPLE BUTTER FROSTING

6 tablespoons butter, softened
½ teaspoon vanilla extract
3½ cups confectioners' sugar
1 teaspoon maple extract
3 tablespoons milk

Combine all ingredients in a large mixing bowl. Beat with an electric mixer until creamy, adding another tablespoon of milk if necessary to achieve a good spreading consistency.

Gem Pans

Gem pans are multi-cup, cast-iron baking pans that have existed in a variety of forms: shallow, deep, round, oval, oblong, rectangular, marked, and unmarked. Their origins can be traced back to nineteenth-century Boston tinplate worker, shop owner, and inventor Nathaniel Waterman. His design was the first to bring together multiple cast-iron baking cups in a single baking pan, connected in such a way as to create heat passages between the cups for uniform baking. However, Waterman's 1859 invention was called an "Egg Pan and Cake Baker," with no mention of the term *gem* included in the patent.

If Waterman didn't *name* the gem pan, who did? The "Gem Pan" name first appeared in 1862, in an advertisement by New York doctor R. T. Trall, promoting THE NEW GEM PAN, his own invention, a shallow, compartmented, pressed tin pan with twelve small squares. The advertisement describes a wholesome bread called "Gems," made from a batter of graham flour and water. In 1863, in Trall's monthly health journal, an editor's note accompanying graham bread recipes says the name "Gem" was applied arbitrarily to one of the bread recipes during a lively discussion among diners at Dr. Trall's residential health institution. These graham gem recipes were published in newspapers throughout the 1860s alongside advertisements for Waterman's patented pan. Soon the names merged, and Waterman's pans became known as gem pans. By the 1870s and for decades afterward, most cookbooks had recipes for gems, both the healthy graham versions and, increasingly over time, more sumptuous gems made with milk, baking powder, butter, sugar, and fruit.

Summarized from "Commonly Called Gem Pans: How the Gem Pan Got Its Name," by food historian Corinne Wetzel. Published in The Wagner and Griswold Society newsletter The Casting Call *21, no. 1 (2024): 6–10*

Giving Back

Many charitable individuals and organizations existed during the Gilded Age, some focused on ensuring that children from poorer families received a bit of Christmas joy. For example, the Brooklyn Christmas Tree Society was first organized by Mrs. Lena Sittig in 1892 to bring holiday cheer to underprivileged children in Brooklyn by treating them to a large Christmas dinner, gifts, and musical performances.

Lena Wilson Sittig was born in 1855 in Philadelphia and moved to Bayonne, New Jersey, as a child, where she was homeschooled by her father. As a young woman, she wrote children's stories that were distributed to nursery schools, and she herself read aloud to delighted groups of young people. She married Frank Sittig in 1877, and the couple soon moved to Brooklyn. She was always sympathetic toward the poor and resolved to devote her life to young children after losing her own child. She started by making pillows and pads for the Brooklyn Seaside Home, then founded the Christmas Tree Society, which continued for almost forty years (even after her death in 1913).

Mrs. Sittig raised money and received donated gifts and assistance from other members of Gilded Age society to make this happen. In 1899 an estimated three thousand people were entertained at her annual event, which was held at two New York locations, the Grand Opera House and the Park Theater, both featuring an appearance from Santa Claus alongside a huge Christmas tree lit by red, white, and blue electric lights. Dinner followed at the Thirteenth Regiment Armory, where gifts ranging from gloves and scarfs to dolls, books, and toys were distributed to the children. The Brooklyn Rapid Transit Company provided free transportation, and the orchestras of the two theaters contributed their services. The entertainers, including singers, a sleigh bell soloist, and a monkey trainer, also performed without any fee.

Helen Gould, the eldest daughter of railroad industry magnate Jay Gould and Helen Day Miller Gould, was another wealthy Gilded Age woman well known for her annual Christmas season charity. She famously provided a yearly Christmas feast to her employees at Lyndhurst, her Tarrytown, New York, residence. The 1899 menu printed in the Rochester, New York, *Democrat and Chronicle* featured soup, roast turkey, white and sweet potatoes, peas, tomatoes, onions, corn, chicken salad, mince pie, plum pudding, ice cream, fruit, nuts, coffee, and milk. Another notable charitable event was funding a free Christmas dinner in 1892 for children living in New York's Home for the Friendless, featuring goodies such as chicken, mince pie, nuts, oranges, and candy. In 1900 she provided a Christmas dinner, gifts, and a large fir tree decked out in electric lights, strings of popcorn, and other ornaments for disabled children at Irvington-on-the-Hudson in 1900, as well as a large Christmas tree, turkey dinner, and gifts including skates, clothing, candy, books, and toys for the boys at the Woody Crest Home for Boys in Tarrytown, New York.

Helen Gould and her niece in the sunroom on the Veranda at Lyndhurst, 1905. LYNDHURST MANSION COLLECTION

Christmas at Woody Crest, 1905. LYNDHURST MANSION COLLECTION

Lemon Gingerbread

Gingerbread cake was a common feature in Gilded Age holiday celebrations, largely due to the introduction of baking powder and other chemical leavenings in the nineteenth century, which led to the development of soft gingerbread or gingerbread cake. As a result, in America, the term gingerbread *often became associated with gingerbread cakes. In researching a variety of period recipes, I landed on this version, which is actually a combination of four different nineteenth-century recipes. All called for lemon as an ingredient—both the zest and juice—as well as molasses and brandy; it was a matter of trying different combinations to allow the ingredients to mesh correctly. Ginger and cayenne pepper were common additions at the time, and they provide a nice, spicy kick. Some recipes called for no sugar at all (just molasses for sweetening), but I found just a little brown sugar provided some sweetness to balance the tartness of the lemon.*

 MAKES ONE 9-INCH SQUARE CAKE (ABOUT 16 SERVINGS) 

6 tablespoons unsalted butter
1 cup molasses
¼ cup dark brown sugar
¼ cup lemon juice, strained
1 tablespoon lemon zest
¼ cup brandy

2 cups all-purpose flour
½ teaspoon salt
1½ teaspoons ginger
2 teaspoons baking soda
⅛ teaspoon cayenne pepper

Preheat the oven to 375°F. Grease a square 9-inch pan.

Combine the butter, molasses, and brown sugar in a heavy-bottomed pot over low heat. When they are melted, remove from heat and add the lemon juice, zest, and brandy.

Stir with a wire whisk until well mixed. Sift the flour with the salt, ginger, baking soda, and cayenne pepper in another bowl. Add to the wet ingredients in the pot a little at a time until no lumps remain.

Pour the batter into the pan and smooth the top. Bake on the middle rack for 25–30 minutes.

Let cool on a wire rack. When completely cool, cut into squares. Sprinkle with confectioners' sugar if desired.

Dominoes

These delightful bite-size treats were little cakes designed to literally look like domino game pieces. Baked in a thin layer in a sheet pan, the cake was cut into oblong-shaped pieces when cool and then decorated to resemble dominos. Some versions had chocolate icing and white dots. Other recipes called for white frosting accented with chocolate dots, like this recipe adapted from Sarah Tyson Rorer. They were especially beloved by children and were often served at children's Christmas parties, arranged on a dish embellished with colorful tissue paper cut into frills.

MAKES 2 DOZEN TREATS

1 stick (½ cup) butter, softened
1 cup sugar
2 eggs, separated
1 teaspoon lemon extract
2 cups flour
2 teaspoons baking powder
½ teaspoon salt
¾ cup milk
½ cup chocolate chips

Preheat oven to 350°F. Grease a rectangular 9 × 13 × 2-inch pan.

Cream butter and sugar in a large mixing bowl with an electric mixer on medium-high speed until pale yellow in color. Add the egg yolks (reserve whites for the icing) and lemon extract and mix until combined.

Sift the flour with the baking powder and salt in another bowl. With the mixer set to a low speed, add the dry ingredients to the butter mixture, alternating with the milk until well blended.

Pour the batter into the pan, smoothing the top. (It will be a thin layer.) Bake for about 20 minutes or until a toothpick inserted in the center comes out clean. Set on a wire rack to cool. While the cake is cooling, make the icing.

VANILLA BOILED ICING

2 egg whites
1⅓ cups granulated sugar
⅓ cup water
½ teaspoon vanilla

Using an electric mixer, beat the egg whites in a large glass or stainless steel bowl on high speed until soft peaks form, about 3–4 minutes. Set aside.

Make a syrup by combining the sugar and water in a heavy-bottomed pot. Bring to a boil and boil for 5 minutes without stirring.

Pour the syrup over the beaten whites in a thin stream while beating constantly. Add the vanilla and continue beating until very stiff and a spreadable consistency, about 10–15 minutes.

When Dominoes are cool, frost with the boiled icing. Then melt ½ cup chocolate chips in a glass bowl in the microwave in 30-second increments, stirring well in between. Create a dot pattern on top of each Domino by dipping a small brush in the melted chocolate or placing a bit of chocolate on the edge of a spoon and gently pushing a little off with a toothpick onto the cake and swirling into a circle.

Children's Christmas dinner party, 1897, Griffith & Griffith, Publisher. LIBRARY OF CONGRESS

Black Women's Clubs

The Gilded Age was a time for change as well as innovation. Women's organizations such as New York's Sorosis Club and Philadelphia's New Century Club encouraged freethinking, creativity, and charitable work among women and the promotion of science, literature, and art in a comfortable and convenient meeting place. The women's suffrage movement also helped push the needle for women, enabling them to air and share their thoughts more freely, exchange ideas, and rally together.

However, women's club members were primarily white, middle-class women. So African American women began forming their own groups. Created in 1893, the Ida B. Wells Club was the first of these trailblazing organizations, championed by former schoolteacher Ida B. Wells. The club started by sponsoring a kindergarten for Black students and quickly threw their efforts behind many other groups, such as reading rooms, youth clubs, and social settlements. Many clubs followed suit, with volunteers providing both their time and money for all kinds of groups from less-privileged walks of life, founding homes for orphans, working women, and the elderly. They funded items like toys, food, clothing, and heating for the facilities. They also presented plays and sponsored musicals, raffles, picnics, and balls to raise money for building repairs, furniture, groceries, and other necessities. Many members also volunteered their time organizing Christmas parties for the orphaned children.

Christmas Cake

Christmas cake began appearing in the mid-nineteenth century. Essentially, it was a more cake-like version of plum pudding, omitting alcohol as an ingredient to make it more suitable for family gatherings. By the Gilded Age, there were several variations. Although most featured lemon as a flavoring in some form, some were baked in the fashion of a yellow cake, rich with butter, sugar, eggs, and cream, and others were laden with lots of dried fruit and maybe some nuts and/or anise seed. Then there were versions that were in between these two styles, such as the recipe featured below. Some cookbooks recommended making small Christmas cakes that could be decorated with "fanciful designs," such as a flower (made from a candied cherry as the center and split almonds as the petals) or a turtle (crafted using a large raisin as the center and some whole cloves as the head and feet).

2 sticks (1 cup) butter, softened
1 cup sugar
3 eggs
1 teaspoon lemon extract
3 cups flour
1 teaspoon cinnamon
½ teaspoon nutmeg
2 teaspoons baking powder
1 cup raisins
½ cup dried currants
¼ cup diced candied citron*
1 cup milk

Preheat oven to 350°F. Grease and flour a 9- to 10-inch Bundt pan (or two 6-inch ones).

Cream the butter and sugar in a bowl until a pale yellow color, about 1–2 minutes. Add the eggs one at a time, continuing to beat until well mixed, then add lemon extract. Sift the flour with the cinnamon, nutmeg, and baking powder in a separate bowl, then stir in the dried fruit. Gradually add to the butter, sugar, and egg mixture, alternating with the milk. Mix until thoroughly combined.

Pour batter into the Bundt pan(s). Place on the oven's center rack and bake for about 50–60 minutes for a full-sized pan or 35–40 minutes for two smaller ones, or until a toothpick inserted in the center comes out clean. Place pan on a wire rack to cool, about 10–20 minutes, then place another wire rack over the base of the cake and invert the pan to release the cake. You may need to run a knife along the pan edges and/or tap the sides.

Christmas Cake

CONTINUED

* Diced candied citron can be found in the baking section of grocery stores or online. Paradise is a brand commonly used.

When cool, drizzle with Lemon Vanilla Glaze.

LEMON VANILLA GLAZE

1 cup confectioners' sugar

2 tablespoons lemon juice

1 teaspoon vanilla

Place all ingredients in a small bowl and mix with a wire whisk until combined. Drizzle on the cake with a spoon. If you want an extra punch, use a toothpick or wooden skewer to poke several holes in the top of the cake before applying the glaze; some of the sugary glaze will infuse the cake with moisture and sweetness.

This cake is best served the day it is made. Refrigerate any leftover cake and heat in the microwave for 30–60 seconds before serving, if desired.

CITRON

Native to northeast India, citron is a citrus fruit that resembles a large, rustic-looking lemon, with a much thicker rind and a more bitter taste than oranges and lemons. Typically known as one of the oldest citrus fruits and the first to make its way to Europe, citron became a kind of catchall term for all citrus fruits. The rind is especially fragrant and aromatic, and it was incorporated into many baked goods such as fruitcake, coffee cake, hot cross buns, and Christmas stollen (cake) in dried, candied form, often used in tandem with other dried fruits. In the Gilded Age, cooks and bakers would often have to do the preserving themselves, which could be a lengthy process, involving removing the rind, drying it, and then soaking it and boiling it in a sugary syrup before placing it in the sun to dry. The hollow rinds were filled with sugar and set out to "remain in the hottest sunshine for as many days as required to dry thoroughly, filling the hollows every few days with sugar." Luckily citron can be purchased already candied and chopped today!

Fudgy Chocolate Cake

Chocolate cakes started popping up on Christmas menus toward the end of the Gilded Age, and by the early 1900s there were many different types, with colorful names such as Midnight Cake, Devil's Cake, and Fudge Cake. Some had chocolate icing, and some called for white icing, an interesting contrast to the dark chocolate interior. Multilayer versions sometimes integrated chocolate with other contrasting cake types (such as white cake with orange flavoring) and various fillings to sandwich between the layers, ranging from a rich brown sugar caramel to a light and fluffy chocolate whipped cream, as featured in the recipe below. Butter-cream frostings began appearing around this time too, often as a replacement for boiled icings.

SERVES 12

3 ounces unsweetened baking chocolate
1 stick (½ cup) salted butter, softened
1¼ cups dark brown sugar
1 teaspoon vanilla
2 eggs
2 cups flour
1½ teaspoons baking powder
½ teaspoon baking soda
1 cup milk

Preheat oven to 350°F. Grease and flour two 9-inch round baking pans (or spray and line with parchment paper). Place a mixing bowl and beaters in the freezer (for making the cream filling).

Place the chocolate in a microwave-safe dish and heat in the microwave on high for 30 seconds. Take out the dish and give the chocolate a stir. Continue doing this in 30-second intervals until chocolate is melted. Set aside.

With an electric mixer, cream butter and sugar in a bowl until blended. Add vanilla and then eggs, one at a time, beating well after each addition. Gradually add the melted chocolate until thoroughly incorporated.

Sift the flour with the baking powder and soda in a separate bowl. Add these dry ingredients to the first mixture, alternating with the milk, continuing to mix until a smooth batter is formed, scraping down sides of bowl as needed.

Fudgy Chocolate Cake

CONTINUED

Divide the batter evenly between the two pans, smoothing the top. Place in the oven on the middle rack and bake for 20–25 minutes or until a toothpick inserted in the center comes out clean. Cool on a wire rack for about 10 minutes, then loosen from the pans by running a sharp knife or spatula around the edges and inverting on wire racks. Let cool completely.

While the cake is cooling, make the filling and frosting.

FOR THE CHOCOLATE FILLING

1 cup heavy cream

1 teaspoon vanilla

4 tablespoons cocoa powder

¼ teaspoon salt

¾ cup sugar

Remove the mixing bowl and beaters from the freezer. Add all the ingredients and whip with an electric mixer on medium-high speed until firm peaks form, about 2–3 minutes.

FOR THE CHOCOLATE BUTTER FROSTING

1 package (4 ounces) unsweetened chocolate

6 tablespoons unsalted butter, softened

3 cups confectioners' sugar

1 teaspoon vanilla

⅛ teaspoon salt

5–7 tablespoons milk

Place the chocolate in a microwave-safe dish and heat in the microwave on high for 30 seconds. Take out the dish and give the chocolate a stir. Continue doing this in 30-second intervals until chocolate is melted. Set aside.

Fudgy Chocolate Cake

Using an electric mixer, cream the butter and sugar in a large mixing bowl on medium speed until smooth, then add the melted chocolate, vanilla, salt, and 5 tablespoons milk. Mix well and add an additional tablespoon or two of milk if mixture is too thick to spread.

To assemble the cake, place one layer on a plate and spread it with fluffy filling. Top with the other layer and then frost the top, leaving the sides open to show the layers.

Chocolate Cake

It's hard to imagine, but chocolate cake didn't always exist! It wasn't until the mid-nineteenth century that chocolate as a cake flavoring really started appearing in cookbooks. Prior to this, chocolate was consumed mainly as a beverage. In fact, the earliest recipes labeled "chocolate cake" were meant to be eaten with hot chocolate and actually contain no chocolate at all.

But in 1828 a Dutchman by the name of van Houten patented a way to simplify cacao processing by pressing out most of the fat and alkalizing the dry cocoa that remained. This revolutionized chocolate manufacturing, paving the way for all kinds of chocolate dessert possibilities. In the late 1870s improvements in cocoa processing created a much smoother, more delicious tasting chocolate, which better translated to cake baking. By the beginning of the twentieth century, recipes for chocolate cakes began to flourish, largely due to companies like Baker's Chocolate realizing the power of product marketing, partnering with cooking school instructors such as Maria Parloa and Janet McKenzie Hill to publish several recipe pamphlets featuring chocolate desserts.

One of these specialty chocolate cake recipes was for devil's food cake, a dark, moist layer cake frosted with a thick coating of icing. Even more chocolatey and richly hued than a regular chocolate cake, it is the polar opposite of its distant cousin, the fluffy, pure white angel food cake. According to food historians, this is one theory of how the name originated: the two contrasts, light angel food versus sinfully rich devil's food. However, as Greg Patent surmises in *Baking in America*, it could also be from the cake's slightly reddish tint. The red color was thought to be due to a chemical reaction that occurred between early varieties of baking soda and cocoa, which could also gave the cake a soapy taste, notes Dawn Marie Schrandt in *Just Me Cookin' Cakes*. This eventually branched off into the southern favorite, red velvet cake (originally called red devil's cake).

In any case, when recipes for this denser, richer chocolate cake first began appearing in cookbooks, they were called devil's cake, and they were often loaf cakes, not multilayer. By the 1890s recipes for devil's food cake began to emerge, and these two interchangeable names continued through the early part of the twentieth century. By the mid-twentieth century, most of these dark cakes were called devil's food cakes.

How did these cakes obtain their darker color and deeper flavor and texture? Many recipes used molasses, brown sugar, and other spices, enhanced with chocolate filling and frosting. Others just added more chocolate for a richer look and taste and/or used egg yolks instead of whole eggs for a custardy texture; some called for beating the whites separately and then adding them to the batter. One popular early recipe was from Philadelphia Cooking School instructor Sarah Tyson Rorer. Published in *Mrs. Rorer's New Cook Book* in 1902, in it she basically just doubles the amount of chocolate and cooks it with milk until smooth and thick (like a custard) to produce a richer taste. She also specifies pastry flour and warns, "The success of this cake depends on the flour used."

CHAPTER THREE
PIES, PUDDINGS, AND CUSTARDS

The time-honored mince pie ranks first in place as standard Christmas dessert.

GOOD HOUSEKEEPING,
DECEMBER 25, 1886

PIES AND PUDDINGS actually started out as savory fare, with fillings including beef, pigeon, veal and ham, fish and oyster, and potato. Puddings were typically a mix of starch, eggs, milk, and a flavoring cooked in some kind of container, meant to whet the appetite before the more substantial meat course was brought out. Examples included carrot, pea, or potato pudding; cheese pudding; and batter pudding (a simple mix of butter, milk, flour, eggs, and salt). Pies could be open on top (with just a bottom crust) or feature a top crust encasing a variety of fillings. They were a very practical food since they used less flour than bread and could stretch provisions to feed more hungry mouths.

Some pie recipes started to combine sweet and savory components, such as plum pudding and mince pies. Ironically these are also the two desserts that show up the most often on nineteenth-century Christmas menus, which likely stemmed from the fact that the holiday season was deemed a special occasion to use sugar and other more expensive "sweet" ingredients such as dried fruit. In fact, plum pudding could also be called "Christmas pudding" and mince pie was sometimes referred to as "Christmas pie."

Early English colonists brought their love of both puddings and pies to the New World, and when sugar became more available and reasonably priced in

the nineteenth century, sweet pies and puddings quickly became among the most popular desserts in America. The line between them was often blurred, with the two terms used interchangeably. For example, many cream and custard pies such as almond, apple, coconut, lemon, and orange were listed in era cookbooks as puddings, but they were baked in a pie pan lined with a pastry crust or at least rimmed with a strip of pastry. Fruit pies were often a dessert favorite. In *Mrs. Hale's New Cook Book* (1857), Sarah Josepha Hale recommends gooseberries, currants, cherries, raspberries, plums, cranberries, and damsons (small oval plums) for making large pies, with one pound of sugar to a quart of fruit as the proper proportion.

Plum pudding and mince pie continued to reign as the most popular Christmas desserts throughout most of the Gilded Age, but by the early 1900s, other pies and puddings began to be associated with Christmas and other winter holidays. Those listed on era menus included pumpkin, apple, chocolate cream pudding, cottage pudding (a custardy bread pudding with currants or other fruit such as plums, cherries, or berries), Montrose pudding (a frosty two-layer pudding combining vanilla custard and strawberry water ice), and snow pudding (a molded pudding made from lemon or vanilla flavored gelatin and frothed egg whites and served with a rich custard sauce).

LYNDHURST MANSION, TARRYTOWN, NY

The Christmas Tree

The tree that graces modern American homes at Christmas has a long and varied backstory. An 1893 *Good Housekeeping* article traces the origin of the Christmas tree back to central and northern Europe before the introduction and spread of Christianity. The Teuton and Saxon people had a great respect for trees and believed they housed their gods, including Berchta, a benign spirit who took care of babies, rocking them to sleep. To show their devotion, they decorated the trees with lights, wreaths, and tassels and hung offerings in the branches when they held festivals to celebrate the gods.

Eventually Germans began to set up and decorate a tree with treats and small gifts on it inside their homes during the Christmas season, a tradition that made its way to America. By the Gilded Age, many people had a Christmas tree in their parlors as a holiday decoration, at first hanging small gifts from its branches and then placing them under the tree as Christmas gifts began to grow in size and became too heavy to hang on the tree. Because the tree was given such a central position in the household, it showcased the family gift exchange and focused everyone's attention on giving and receiving.

In the Gilded Age, trees were often decorated with beautiful shiny glass ornaments, which were available for purchase in many toy shops. Homemade ornaments were also popular, made out of cardboard or paper cut into festive shapes and covered with gold or brightly colored paper. And fruit or nuts were sometimes painted a golden color, or covered with gold paper, and hung on the tree with colored ribbon. Strings of popcorn or cranberries were intertwined among the tree branches to serve as decorative garlands.

Before electric lights were introduced, Christmas trees were illuminated by the glow of real candles attached to tree branches, typically set in holders that had a weighted, colored ball at the lower end to help keep the candle upright. According to *The Young Folk's Cyclopædia of Games and Sports* (1890), "Each candle should be lighted and allowed to burn a few seconds before putting it in place. In placing the candles, it should be seen that all loose things above them are trimmed off, so that there is no danger of fire." This book also suggests having one or two extra candles on hand to help light the candles, and a sponge or rag saturated with water to extinguish any that appeared likely to set fire to the tree. (Yikes!) At least this role was deemed important enough to "be the sole business of one person, while the tree remains lighted, to take charge of the sponge, and each candle, as it burns down into the socket, should be put out." A tree six feet tall averaged about fifty candles, and a very stately tree of twelve feet high could hold a staggering four hundred candles.

Merry Christmas holiday postcard. NEW YORK PUBLIC LIBRARY DIGITAL COLLECTION

Presents and Where to Put Them

Unlike today, Christmas presents were often hung on the tree, tied to the branches by strings or ribbons, which were cut by the recipient. Each present was clearly marked with the name of the giver and the receiver and read aloud when they were taken down from the tree. Sometimes a ladder served as a substitute for the Christmas tree. First it was adorned with evergreen and other festive holiday branches, then the presents, candles, and ornaments were fastened to the rungs, hung just as if on a tree. Another unusual tradition was hanging presents on a toy ship (typically purchased at a toy shop) instead of on a tree. The presents were placed inside the ship and hung on the masts and rigging, which were strung with garlands of greens and decorated with taper candles. Some folks even went a step further and displayed the ship to look like it was sailing on the water (represented by green cloth). In this case, the presents were stowed in a box underneath the ship and taken out through the hatchways on Christmas morning.

Bran Pie

An English Christmas gift custom was the bran pie. Similar to the gag gifts some folks like to exchange today, this "pie" was simply a large dish filled with novelty, inexpensive Christmas presents, such as pincushions, needle-cases, change purses, bonbons, books, balls, and little toys, each wrapped in paper and hidden by covering it with bran. The pie was brought to the Christmas dinner table after dessert, as the last and crowning dish of the feast. Just before the pie was "served," each person was given a new plate and spoon. And then with great fanfare, the host would say: "We have here a bran pie. As it is passed around, let each one help oneself." Each person would then dig into the pie with a spoon and retrieve one item. Once everyone at the table had a present, they would all open their gifts at the same time, complete with jokes and commentary, adding "an agreeable half-hour to the Christmas dinner table," according to an 1891 *American Notes and Queries* article.

When this custom carried over into America's Gilded Age, the bran pie was often placed on the table on Christmas morning. It was the same concept: small presents wrapped in paper were hidden in the bottom of a large pan and covered with bran or sawdust. However, sometimes the top was covered with a real pie crust and browned in the oven (in this case, none of the presents were flammable or otherwise sensitive to heat—a pretty crazy idea!). Another (safer) way was using thick brown paper to simulate the crust. When the pie was placed on the table, part of the "crust" was removed and the presents were lifted out of the bran, one by one.

Orange Tartlets

The rapid expansion of rail lines during the Gilded Age drove large-scale commercialization of oranges in Florida and California. As a result, oranges as a dessert food proliferated during the era. There were even special serving dishes and cutlery for eating them, either whole or halved. For Christmas dinner, oranges showed up in a variety of desserts, including orange sherbet, Christmas orange cake, orange pudding, and these delightful orange tarts, reminiscent of miniature orange meringue pies.

YIELDS FOUR 4-INCH TARTS OR SIX 3-INCH TARTS

FOR THE CRUST

1¼ cup all-purpose flour

½ teaspoon salt

1 stick (½ cup) cold unsalted butter

4–5 tablespoons cold water

Sift together the flour and salt in a large mixing bowl. Cut in half of the butter with a pastry blender or two knives until evenly mixed and the consistency of coarse sand. Cut in the remaining butter and blend until the dough is in pea-sized pieces.

Add the water a little at a time, stirring lightly with a fork. Use only as much water as you need to make the dough hold together. Form the dough into a circle about an inch thick and wrap in plastic wrap or waxed paper. Chill in the refrigerator for 30 minutes. While dough is chilling, make the orange filling.

FOR THE FILLING

2 large navel oranges

1 tablespoon unsalted butter

3 eggs, separated

½ cup sugar, plus 3 tablespoons

1 tablespoon flour

¼ teaspoon salt

Preheat oven to 375°F.

Grate the rinds of both oranges with a zester or other fine grater to yield 1 tablespoon orange zest. Juice the oranges, straining through a fine sieve to yield ⅔ cup. Combine the juice, zest, butter, 3 egg yolks, ½ cup sugar, flour, and salt in a small saucepan. Cook over low heat until slightly thickened. Remove from heat and set aside.

Orange Tartlets

To make the tart crust, place dough on a lightly floured surface and roll into a ⅛-inch-thick circle. Cut out circles to fit the tart pans you are using. Line tart pans with dough, then fill each with orange mixture. Bake for 25 minutes or until filling is set.

While tarts are baking, make the meringue topping by beating 3 egg whites in a large glass or stainless steel bowl with an electric mixer on low until foamy, about 3–4 minutes. Slowly add 3 tablespoons sugar and keep beating, increasing speed to medium-high, until whites form fluffy, firm peaks that curl slightly at their tips when the beater is raised.

When the tarts are done, remove from the oven and spread meringue over each, making a swirly pattern. Return to the oven and bake for 5–8 minutes or until nicely browned on top. Remove pan from oven and tarts from pan and let cool on a wire rack for 1 hour, then refrigerate until ready to serve.

Some Elaborate Orange Desserts

Gilded Age cookbooks and magazine articles abound with elegant ways to serve oranges. In one extra-fancy presentation, orange segments were scooped out and juiced to make a sparkling gelatin, which was dyed in a range of colors and then placed inside the orange rind, which had been cut into a basket shape. Another serving method called for cutting large oranges in half, scooping out the fruit, and dicing it into small pieces. The fruit was then sprinkled with sugar and coconut and placed inside half of the orange "shells." The other halves were filled with orange water ice or ice cream, and the two halves were tied together side by side with a white satin ribbon through holes made near the top of each shell. Yet a third dessert was tangerine creams, which called for cutting holes in the tops of six tangerines and scooping out the pulp with a tiny spoon, leaving the rind whole and intact. The cream was made by squeezing the tangerine juice and mixing it with a pint of cream, the pulp, some sugar, and plain gelatin. It was then poured into the scooped out tangerines and set on ice or in a cold place. After a few hours, the top halves were carefully peeled away with a knife to reveal the orange ice cream sitting inside an attractive tangerine cup. The tops were then garnished with thin strips of lemon peel.

Road of a Thousand Wonders

through California and Oregon over the Southern Pacific

The Orange in your Christmas Stocking

comes from the land of a thousand wonders – of midwinter flowers and midwinter golden fruit, of midwinter bathing in the sea, of midwinter motoring, golf and tennis and mountains of midwinter green, of giant trees to picnic under, in midwinter; of more than a thousand attractions.

BULL

Advertisement from Red Book *magazine, 1905.* GOOGLE BOOKS

Christmas Oranges

Although ubiquitous in markets today, before the days of fast transport such as steamships and trains, oranges and other exotic fruits were an expensive, highly coveted status symbol. Most required warmer climates to grow, and unless one had access to a hothouse, they were almost impossible to obtain. As the world became more global, access to fresh fruit out of season (including oranges in Northern Europe and/or North America) was possible, but still rare. This made these items perfect Christmas gifts, and they were often placed in the toe of children's Christmas stockings as a special treat.

Charitable groups frequently made sure that it wasn't only children from upper-class homes who enjoyed this luxury. A 1907 article titled "Christmas Stockings" in the publication *What to Eat* discusses filling stockings "for children who live in homes that Santa Claus seems 'to forget.'" The article suggests buying a dozen pairs of stockings and filling one stocking of each pair with gifts such as candy, nuts, an orange, and an apple, and then attaching the unfilled stockings (the "mates") to the filled ones so that "there are gifts enough to make as many children happy with an answer from Santa Claus, as you have purchased pairs of stockings."

The idea behind putting oranges in stockings also extended to May baskets, a custom of hanging baskets with offerings to one's friends during the month of May. These baskets were hung up overnight on a friend's doorknob, where the recipient would find them in the morning. This tradition started as a way to give flowers but eventually extended to include gifts such as fruit, candy, and other goodies. An 1899 *Good Housekeeping* article suggests making a stocking out of white netting trimmed with flowers and including a doll made from an orange wrapped in white tissue paper (for the head), set on top of a jam jar filled with nuts and candy to serve as the body, which was then covered with tissue paper to simulate a shawl and skirt.

Meringues de Pomme

Also known as meringued apples or apples meringue, this is a delicious baked apple dish with a light, airy meringue topping. The contrasting texture of pillowy, slightly crispy meringue balances the warm spiced apples perfectly. A sweet blend of stiffly beaten egg whites and sugar, meringue was a popular feature in many nineteenth-century desserts. The Philadelphia Housewife *(1855) cookbook cleverly recommended swirling a peak of meringue over each apple so it stands out for serving.*

SERVES 6

6 medium apples
2 teaspoons sugar
1 teaspoon cinnamon
3 tablespoons butter
2 tablespoons orange marmalade or apricot jam
4 egg whites, at room temperature
Pinch of cream of tartar
4 tablespoons confectioners' sugar
½ tablespoon rosewater
Slivered almonds, for garnish (optional)

Preheat oven to 350°F. Butter a deep 2-quart baking dish or coat with cooking spray.

Peel and core the apples and set them upright in the baking dish. Pour ⅓ cup water into the bottom of the dish to prevent the apples from burning as they bake. Combine sugar and cinnamon in a small bowl. Put about ½ teaspoon of the cinnamon-sugar mixture and a pat (½ tablespoon) of butter into the center of each apple. Bake until just tender, about 30–40 minutes.

While the apples are baking, make a meringue by beating the egg whites in a large glass or stainless steel bowl with an electric mixer on low until foamy, about 3–4 minutes. Add cream of tartar, increase speed to medium, and continue beating until whites form softly curling peaks. Slowly add the confectioners' sugar and rosewater and keep beating, increasing speed to medium-high, until whites form fluffy, firm peaks that curl slightly at their tips when the beater is raised.

When the apples are done, remove the dish from the oven and carefully drain off any excess juice. Fill the cores with a teaspoon of marmalade or jam. Cover the apples

Meringues de Pomme

with the meringue, beginning at the top of each apple and then spreading it down evenly with a broad-bladed spreader or knife until it is smooth and of equal thickness all over the top of the apples.

Return the dish to the oven for 5–8 minutes until lightly browned on the top. Serve while still warm, or cool completely and refrigerate until ready to serve. Pair with a scoop of vanilla ice cream or whipped cream if desired. Garnish with a sprinkling of slivered almonds if desired.

Christmas Décor

Gilded Age women were not at a loss when deciding how to decorate their homes for Christmas. Books and magazines offered a variety of suggestions for décor, particularly when planning Christmas dinner. *Table Talk* magazine suggested placing a circular mat in the center of the table, embroidered with sprays of holly and berries around its edges, with matching doilies. To continue the festive look, paper candle shades were replaced with Christmas greenery, and a round mirrored base strewn with stray leaves and blossoms held low dishes of ferns, scarlet geraniums and white carnations, eupatoria (herbs with white or purple flowers), or other snow-white flowers.

Other ideas included placing boughs of holly tied with red satin ribbon at each corner of the table, so they met in the center to form a pyramid of holly sprigs, snowballs, and bright red candy shavings, flanked by candelabras with red candles. As noted in a 1905 *Country Life in America* article, "[The lady of the house] will want the smell of cedar and the gleam of red berries and glossy leaves to greet her household when they come in. She will want a bit of mistletoe to preserve certain hoary, time-honored jokes, and she would have a Yule-log if she could."

In *Mrs. Rorer's Everyday Menu Book* (1905), food writer and cooking school instructor Sarah Tyson Rorer recommended using either a combination of holly, cedar, and mistletoe or ground pine and partridge berry. In order to get the best greenery, she suggested seeking out Christmas greens a week or two ahead and storing them in a cool, damp place until it was time to decorate. Holly branches with an abundance of large red berries were the most desirable, particularly those given a sprinkling of frost powder. She specifically stated not to use roses or other hothouse flowers, as "they are entirely inappropriate." This statement was mainly directed to middle-class families, since flowers were very costly during the holiday season. As she explained, "At Christmas time, when the spirit of giving is upon us, we hesitate to squander our substance upon these perishable luxuries, when the amount expended upon them might carry Christmas cheer of a more substantial sort into a number of homes. But it is possible to arrange a very charming table without them."

There was also festive and charming holiday décor geared for children's Christmas dinner tables. In a 1905 *Ladies Home Journal* article titled "Christmas Tables and Christmas Dishes," one photo depicts a tablescape designed to imitate a snowstorm. Wire covered with artificial snow was strung through the chandelier above the table and tied with puffs of cotton. A reindeer was poised on a block of ice

Street vendor selling Christmas greens, Puck, 1897. LIBRARY OF CONGRESS

sprinkled with crystal snow. Candles placed around the table featured white shades with fringes of snowflakes decorated with holly. At each place setting, a plate of snowball cookies served as Christmas favors. This article also suggested creating a centerpiece featuring Santa emerging from the top of a chimney, crafted by covering a box with red paper and using white chalk to mark lines on it to simulate a chimney. A Santa figurine with his pack of toys was placed on top, and little stockings filled with Christmas goodies were arranged around the chimney's edge. Another table idea featured Santa and his reindeer crossing a frozen lake lined with cotton and framed by four tiny pine trees decorated with white taper candles and crystal "icicles" to replicate a winter forest. Santa's sleigh was filled with candies that were given to children as Christmas favors.

Pumpkin Custard

Thought to have originated in Central America, pumpkins were abundant throughout North America by the time Europeans began to explore the New World and were a common ingredient in Indigenous American cuisine. Early English settlers used pumpkins in a variety of different preparations (including stewed and in puddings and pies). The meringue topping on this custardy mix of pumpkin, eggs, milk or cream, sweetener, and spices provides an elegant twist to this dessert, which frequently appeared on Gilded Age Christmas dinner menus.

SERVES 10–12

3 eggs, separated
¾ cup sugar, plus 3 tablespoons
1½ cups milk
½ teaspoon salt
1½ teaspoon cinnamon
1 teaspoon ginger
3 cups (one 29-ounce can) pumpkin

Preheat oven to 350°F. Butter a 2-quart baking dish or coat with cooking spray. Set aside.

Separate eggs, reserving whites for meringue topping. Using an electric mixer, beat egg yolks with sugar on medium speed for about 1 minute. Turn mixer to low and slowly add milk, salt, cinnamon, and ginger and mix until combined. Stir in pumpkin, mixing until thick and custardy.

Spoon mixture into the baking dish and bake for about 1 hour or until a toothpick inserted into the center comes out clean.

While the custard is baking, make the meringue topping by beating egg whites in a large glass or stainless steel bowl with an electric mixer on low until foamy, about 3–4 minutes. Slowly add 3 tablespoons sugar and keep beating, increasing speed to medium-high, until whites form fluffy, firm peaks that curl slightly at their tips when the beater is raised.

When the custard is done, remove from the oven and spread meringue over the surface, making a swirly pattern. Return to the oven and bake for 5–10 minutes or until nicely browned on top. Remove from oven and let cool on a wire rack for 1 hour, then refrigerate until ready to serve.

Bakewell Pudding

Also called a Bakewell tart, this is one of the many British recipes that made their way to America. This dessert is famous in the Derbyshire town of Bakewell as well as other counties in northern England, where it is served as a holiday treat. Although it was custardy at first, it later evolved into more of a pudding that sits on top of one layer of ground or chopped almonds and another of strawberry (or other fruit) jam, encased in a puffy pastry crust. By the Gilded Age, it was often served at American Christmas gatherings, particularly by families of British heritage.

SERVES 8–10

1 frozen puff pastry sheet (like Pepperidge Farm), defrosted

½ cup raspberry or strawberry preserves

¼ cup sliced almonds

1 teaspoon lemon zest

1 stick (½ cup) butter, softened

¾ cup sugar

3 large eggs, beaten

1 teaspoon almond extract

Confectioners' sugar (for garnish)

Preheat oven to 350°F. Grease an 8-inch pie pan.

Roll out the pastry on a lightly floured board or counter to about ¼ inch thickness. Place in the pie pan and crimp the edges.

Spoon the preserves into the pie shell, spreading them around evenly to create a bottom layer. Combine the almonds and lemon zest and scatter over the preserves. Set aside.

Place the butter and sugar in a large mixing bowl. Beat using an electric mixer on medium-high speed until creamy, about 2–3 minutes. Reduce speed to medium and add the eggs and almond extract. Continue mixing until smooth. Pour the custard mixture over the preserves and smooth the top.

Bake for 45–50 minutes until nicely brown and the custard is set. Remove from the oven and cool on a wire rack for about 30 minutes, then place in the refrigerator until ready to serve. Just before serving, sprinkle with confectioners' sugar. Serve with ice cream or whipped cream if desired.

Mock Mince Pie

Mincemeat pie stems from England's medieval ages, where it originated as a small pie called a chewette. It typically contained a mixture of dried fruits, chopped nuts and apples, suet and/or minced beef, spices, and lemon juice, vinegar, or brandy. But like many foods, it evolved over time, so when it made its way to America, it was often baked into a large pie to serve several people. In addition, mock versions began to crop up. "Mock" dishes actually go back to the Middle Ages as creative workarounds for the original versions; in the case of mock mincemeat, crackers (and/or sometimes green tomatoes) substituted for meat. This recipe originally called for Uneeda biscuits, which were introduced by the National Biscuit Company (Nabisco) in 1898 and beloved by many until they were discontinued in 2009. Cream crackers are a good alternative.

FOR THE PIECRUST

2 cups all-purpose flour

1 teaspoon salt

1½ sticks (¾ cup) cold unsalted butter

6–7 tablespoons cold water

Lightly stir the flour and salt in a large mixing bowl. Cut in half of the butter with a pastry blender or two knives until evenly mixed and the consistency of coarse sand. Cut in the remaining butter and blend until the dough is in pea-sized pieces.

Add the water a little at a time, stirring lightly with a fork. Use only as much water as you need to make the dough hold together. Form the dough into two circles about an inch thick, one slightly larger than the other, and wrap in plastic wrap or waxed paper. Chill in the refrigerator for 30 minutes.

Place the larger disk of dough on a lightly floured surface and roll into a ⅛-inch-thick circle. Place in a 9-inch pie pan. Line the crust with a piece of parchment paper or aluminum foil and fill the inside with pie weights (either store-bought or dry beans or grains). Chill the crust in the refrigerator for another 30 minutes.

Mock Mince Pie

CONTINUED

FOR THE FILLING

6 cream crackers* (½ cup crushed)
1 cup raisins
½ cup currants
½ cup diced citron**
1 egg, beaten
⅓ cup molasses
½ cup apple or white grape juice
½ cup sugar
Juice and zest of 1 medium lemon
½ teaspoon cinnamon

Preheat oven to 375°F.

Place the crackers in a large plastic storage bag and roll back and forth over them with a rolling pin until crushed into crumbs. (Alternatively, place in a food processer and process until crumbs.) Transfer the crumbs to a large bowl. Add the remaining ingredients and mix together with a wooden spoon until well blended.

To make the pie, spoon the filling into bottom pie crust and add the top crust. Use the smaller circle of pastry for the top crust. Roll it into a circle and roll it onto the rolling pin to transfer to the pie, placing it centrally over the filling. Make a few slashes on the surface with a sharp knife to let steam escape, then crimp the edges.

Alternatively, make a lattice crust by cutting the smaller circle of pastry into ½-inch strips with a sharp knife or pastry cutter. Place strips on top of the pie about 1¼ inches apart across the filling. Trim strips and then press to seal, moistening edges as needed. Turn the pie and do the same thing again so strips crisscross the first layer. Turn overhanging strips down and seal and flute edges by pinching pastry using one index finger on the inside edge and the index finger and thumb of the other hand to pinch pastry into a curved flute shape.

Bake for 40–45 minutes or until browned on top, placing aluminum foil around the edges after 20 minutes if starting to brown. Cool on a wire rack. Sprinkle with confectioners' sugar if desired right before serving.

** I used Jacob's Cream Crackers. Baker's Cream Crackers is another brand (both available in the British food section of many grocery stores or online). If you can't find them, feel free to use unsalted saltine crackers.*

*** I used Paradise brand, available in the baking aisle of many grocery stores or online. If you can't find it, feel free to use finely chopped dried apricots or pineapple.*

Mincemeat

According to *The Oxford Companion to Food*, mincemeat pies rarely contain meat nowadays. But during the Gilded Age, they most certainly did. "Meat should be boiled and chopped, suet crumbed, raisins stoned, sultanas and currants washed, citron shred, apples pared and minced, sugar and spices weighed and measured, and liquor poured out with deliberate thought-taking, and the ingredients compounded at least a week before the crust is made, that the mixture may ripen and mellow," stated the recipe for mincemeat in *The Ladies Home Cook Book* (1896).

Although the Gilded Age was a time of technology and innovation, it appears some kitchen inventions were still in the future as far as mincemeat preparation was concerned. Making mincemeat by hand was a time-consuming process that began at least ten days before the Christmas feast. Although dried fruit had begun to be mass produced and commercialized, it was often still sticky and clumped together when purchased. As a result, currants had to be rinsed at least four times to loosen them and remove any sediment and insects that might have been lurking in the stickiness, a task that this book recommends not leaving to inexperienced kitchen hires. Raisins also needed to be washed, and the large ones destemmed, cut in half, and seeds removed, "a tedious and sticky business." Citron was scraped, then sliced into thin shavings and diced with a sharp knife.

The meat was typically a solid chunk of beef round. The cook would boil it at the same time that the raisins, currants, and citron were prepared. The next day, the cooked meat and suet were chopped fine and then combined with juicy minced apples, the prepared dried fruit, sugar, and spices such as cinnamon, mace, allspice, nutmeg, cloves, and pepper. These were gently tossed so as not to bruise or crush any of the ingredients. Finally, wine and brandy were added to mellow and preserve the mincemeat.

When it was time to bake the pie, a rich pastry crust was filled with liberal amounts of the mincemeat filling. "When the knife enters the generous bosom of the Christmaspie, the whiff of fragrance escaping from the cut should set every pulse a-beating," stated this recipe. "Everybody, except hopelessly confirmed dyspeptics, should taste mince-pie on Christmas day. If properly made, it is far less harmful than dietetic (and vegetarian) pessimists would persuade us into believing. Grated, or powdered old cheese is a pleasant adjunct to it."

Children's Plum Pudding

We have the British to thank for bringing their love of puddings to America, particularly rich and fruity plum pudding (also called Christmas pudding), which was a central part of Gilded Age holiday celebrations. In fact, it was such an important Christmas tradition that even the poor Cratchit family in Dickens's classic A Christmas Carol *had one on their holiday table. The version below, featured in an 1891* Independent *article titled "Some Christmas Dainties: For Old and Young" by Sara Sedgwick, was specifically meant to be suitable for children. As noted by Ms. Sedgwick, "Although a Christmas dinner seems somewhat incomplete without a plum pudding, many careful mothers hesitate to set this rich and indigestible compound before their children. Perhaps the following simpler pudding, known as 'Children's Plum Pudding,' will prove acceptable in some homes." A sauce (often called hard sauce) made from rum or brandy butter was often added right before serving. This version, based on temperance-movement recipes popular at the time, would also be appropriate for this recipe served to children.*

SERVES 8–10

¾ cup milk
½ cup molasses
¾ cup finely chopped suet (or lard)
½ teaspoon salt
½ teaspoon baking soda
1½ cups flour
1 teaspoon cinnamon
½ teaspoon ground nutmeg
½ teaspoon allspice
¼ teaspoon ground cloves
1 cup raisins
1 cup currants
½ cup finely chopped dried apricots

Combine all ingredients in a large bowl. Stir thoroughly with a wooden spoon and then cover and place in the refrigerator overnight to blend flavors.

The next day, stir batter again to make sure ingredients are well mixed. Coat a 1.5-quart (or 1.6-liter) tin mold or loaf pan with cooking spray. Pour mixture into the mold and cover with foil.

To steam the pudding, place a steamer insert or some crumpled aluminum foil in the bottom of a deep stockpot, then place the mold on top so that it is not touching the bottom. Fill the pot with enough water so that it is two-thirds up the sides. Bring the

Children's Plum Pudding

CONTINUED

water to a boil, then lower it to a simmer, placing the lid on top. Steam the pudding for 4 hours, adding water if necessary.

Remove the pudding mold from the pot and cool for 1 hour on a wire rack. When cool, loosen the edges and carefully turn the pudding out onto a plate.

You can also steam the pudding in a crock pot. Add 2 cups water to cover the bottom of the crock pot, place the mold inside, and close the lid. Steam the pudding for 4 hours on high, then take it out and let it cool for 1 hour on a wire rack. When cool, loosen the edges and carefully turn the pudding out onto a plate.

HARD SAUCE

2 teaspoons cornstarch
2 tablespoons water
2 egg yolks
¼ cup sugar
1 cup milk
1 tablespoon apricot jelly
Pinch of ground nutmeg

Mix cornstarch and water in a small bowl until smooth, then whisk in egg yolks.

Heat sugar and milk in a medium saucepan over medium-high heat. When it begins to boil, turn down to low and add egg yolks and cornstarch, stirring briskly with a whisk to avoid scrambling. Stir until thick and creamy, then take off the burner and mix in jelly and nutmeg.

Mrs. Cratchit entered—flushed, but smiling proudly—with the pudding, like a speckled cannon-ball, so hard and firm, blazing in half of half-a-quarter of ignited brandy, and bedight with Christmas holly stuck into the top.

—CHARLES DICKENS, *A CHRISTMAS CAROL*

Stir-Up Sunday

Modern Americans aren't the only ones to kick off Christmas a bit early; so were folks in the Gilded Age. They had Stir-Up Sunday, which took place on the last Sunday before Advent, sometime during the second half of November. The name actually originated from the prayer of the day heard in church that morning: "Stir-up, we beseech thee, O Lord, the wills of thy faithful people." Over time it also became associated with the stirring of the Christmas (plum) pudding, which began that same week.

On Stir-Up Sunday, all the ingredients for the Christmas pudding were gathered and mixed together, and each family member would take a turn stirring the pudding, from the oldest on down to the youngest. It was believed that anyone who made a wish while stirring the pudding would have their wish come true. The pudding was supposed to be stirred with a wooden spoon in a clockwise direction with eyes closed, or the wish would not be granted. Sometimes the cook would add charms and trinkets while the pudding was being stirred. When the pudding was later served on Christmas day, whoever got the piece of pudding with a charm would have good luck for the year. Examples ranged from a ring (meaning the recipient would soon be married), to a coin (coming into wealth), to a thimble (either a blessed life or spinsterhood, depending on how it was interpreted).

Once all the family members had taken their turn stirring and making a wish, the pudding was placed in the pudding cloth and hung up until Christmas Day. Letting the pudding mature over the weeks until Christmas was beneficial, as it allowed the flavors to blend and deepen. Before serving, it was boiled for four to five hours, then turned out onto a dish, where the warm brandy sauce was poured over it. The pudding was then lit up, and the much-anticipated flaming dish was presented to the table with a flourish.

John Jacob Astor: The Model for Ebenezer Scrooge?

Although John Jacob Astor (1763–1848) died before the Gilded Age began, his rags-to-riches story undeniably helped kick off and popularize the extreme wealth and capitalist mindset that defined the era. Born in Germany, he moved to America in 1783 and made his multi-million-dollar fortune by monopolizing the fur industry and then moving into the role of real estate mogul. While he was still alive, his incredibly successful climb from a poor immigrant to one of the leading economic personalities in America often garnered him praise as an example of the new nation's opportunities.

Even though he was cautious about his reputation, he did not always receive positive feedback. The extreme wealth he accumulated provoked some of his opponents to question his ethics and business methods. When he died, there was a range of disparaging remarks in the press coverage of his passing. In addition, some recent biographies depict him as a "greedy old man who was nothing but the true personification of Ebenezer Scrooge in Charles Dickens's *A Christmas Carol*." As Alexander Emmerich speculates in his 2013 book, *John Jacob Astor and the First American Fortune*, "Was old Ebenezer modeled after Astor?"

When Charles Dickens visited the United States in 1842, New York City was one of his scheduled stops. Wealthy New Yorkers were more than happy to show him a good time, organizing many balls and fancy dinners, including one at the City Hotel (Astor's first foray into the hotel industry), where Dickens dined with Astor (then aged seventy-nine). Although Dickens had good things to say about the American way of life while he was still here, his attitude changed once he arrived back home in London, including expressing his distaste for New York City, its elite class, and the country's excesses in general. The result was a series of anti-American newspaper articles, as well as his famous book *A Christmas Carol*, featuring the elderly, cold-hearted miser Ebenezer Scrooge. Although we may never know the true inspiration; with Astor's vast wealth and often stingy nature, the similarities are there.

Christmas in the White House

In 1889 Benjamin Harrison became the first president to set up a holiday tree inside the White House, for the pleasure of family, staff, and visitors. The tree was especially meant to provide joy for the president's two grandchildren—Ben Harrison McKee and his baby sister Mary—on whom he doted and went to great lengths to amuse. He said, "We shall have an old-fashioned Christmas tree for the grandchildren upstairs, and I shall be their Santa Claus." (Yes, he enthusiastically dressed up as Santa for the children and very much looked the part, with his full beard.)

According to the *New York Times*, the tree was a foxtail hemlock, eight or nine feet tall, "liberally decked with glittering glass balls and pendants, while from the topmost branch to the edge of the square table on which the tree stands, it is showered over with countless strands of gold tinsel. To add to the brilliant effect, the end of every branch is capped with four-sided lanterns of various colors and finished with a long point of shining glass filled with quicksilver." At the base of the tree was a three-foot-high, lifelike Santa Claus with a pack containing dolls, toys, and stockings filled with bonbons. Little Ben received gifts including a mechanical toy train engine, sled, drum, horns, a tiny blackboard with easel, crayons, and parlor croquet. Mary received a set of bedroom furniture for her dolls, jumping jacks, a tiny piano, rocking chairs, stuffed animals, and jewelry.

On Christmas day the candles on the tree were lit between 4:00 and 5:00 p.m., and the children's friends were invited to view it in its glory. Mrs. Caroline Harrison had made sure each member of her husband's staff was remembered with a personal token, and all of the domestic employees were called in to receive gifts from under the tree. Just two years later in 1891, electric lights were first installed in the White House, but President and Mrs. Harrison were afraid of the innovative new technology and "refused to operate [the switches] for fear of a shock."

So electric Christmas tree lights in the White House would have to wait until 1894, when Grover Cleveland was in his second (nonconsecutive term). Cleveland and his young wife (the former Frances Folsom, also the youngest first lady ever) embraced this new technology and became the first US presidential family to replace the decorative candles traditionally used to illuminate the White House tree with a string of red, white, and blue electric lights. According to a *New York*

Times article, before the Cleveland family had dinner, a luncheon was served to the children of cabinet members, who came to the White House to see the tree displayed in the second floor Oval Room, then used as a parlor and library. President and Mrs. Cleveland gifted turkeys to the White House employees and gave all the servants generous monetary gifts. After the guests went home, the president dined with his two young daughters, Ruth and Esther; his wife Frances; and her mother, Mrs. Emma Folsom Perrine. They feasted on fresh duck, killed by the president himself on a recent hunting trip to South Carolina.

Mrs. Cleveland was adored by the public and known for her kind and generous nature, which included giving money and personalized Christmas gifts to all the White House servants. In 1888 she participated in a charity dinner at the National Rifles' Armory for the Children's Christmas Club. The meal served to six hundred less-fortunate children included turkey, ice cream, and cake. After dinner the children went upstairs, where a Christmas tree had been erected on the stage and decorated with an array of sparkling ornaments and toys piled underneath, each wrapped in a paper bag and tagged with a brightly colored Christmas card, which were distributed to each child by "Santa Claus." Later they were treated to music played by a section of the Marine Band and a Punch and Judy show, which "delighted the little folks immensely."

Bonbon assortment. COURTESY OF SHANE CONFECTIONERY, PHILADELPHIA, PA

CHAPTER FOUR

CANDIES AND OTHER CONFECTIONS

Candy-making has become as much a feature of the holiday preparations as the distinctive cooking.
—KATHERINE E. MEGEE, *COLLIER'S WEEKLY*, 1902

Lemon Drops
Raisin Penuche
Sugar Plums
Popcorn Balls
Doughnut Hole Croquembouche
Hot Chocolate

DURING THE GILDED AGE, a range of candies and other treats became popularly associated with Christmas. There was an emphasis on bite-sized, individual treats, likely to mirror the seasonal gifts given on Christmas Day. For example, sorbet was often served in miniature yule logs alongside individual plum puddings. Ice cream was presented in diminutive Christmas trees made from confectionery.

Candies such as striped and clear candy sticks, barley sugar, chocolate creams, and gumdrops were "pretty for the table and older people like them for the sake of long-ago Christmases," stated a 1904 magazine article from *Country Life in America*. This article also claimed these candies were "not bad for children" if served alongside more wholesome treats such as raisins and almonds that contribute to a "child's happiness."

And as previously mentioned, the Gilded Age was the time chocolate confections really began to take off, due to the cacao defatting process invented by van Houten. It took several decades, but eventually a market emerged for the cocoa butter obtained from the cocoa bean: candy bars! Britain's Cadbury Brothers began to market chocolate bars in 1842, and Swiss chocolatier Nestle started manufacturing milk chocolate in 1876. Once this process was perfected, combined with a drop in the price of sugar, it allowed chocolate candies to became more affordable and available, so they were included in many Christmas stockings.

Other Chocolate candies and their techniques were also imported from Europe, particularly England, France, Switzerland, and Austria, during the late nineteenth century. One was nougat, a nutty, chewy candy studded with blanched and dried almonds. In addition to chocolate, there were many different varieties including brown, white, pistachio, and vanilla, with textures that could be either light and airy or firm and crunchy. "American nougat" included dried fruit and was stamped into shapes such as half-moons, rings, squares, and diamonds with a roller press. As European chocolate-making knowledge filtered into the United States during the nineteenth century, chocolate manufacturing rapidly expanded. By the 1870s, chocolate-covered candy and caramels were important American businesses. Walter M. Lowney, a famous candy maker from Boston who specialized in handmade chocolates, made a splash at the Chicago World's Fair in 1893 when he exhibited his wares there.

And ironically, items that we might typically associate with summer fairs and beach vacations today, such as ice cream, popcorn, and candy apples, were popular Christmas treats during the latter part of the Gilded Age. These were often formed into interesting designs and combinations, such as the "Ice Cream with Popcorn" recipe featured in a 1905 *Ladies Home Journal* article, which involved molding vanilla ice cream into a ring shape and placing sugared popcorn in the center and around the base of the mold. Another was "Christmas Bonne Bouches," a colorful display of bright red candied apples served on a stemmed crystal compote dish with white bonbons arranged among them to create an "exceedingly attractive dish."

The Black Elite

During the Gilded Age, Black society had their own aristocracy, a cultured, educated elite class with degrees of social exclusivity like those that existed among the white community. Some were free Blacks from old families with long-standing ties to cities such as Philadelphia, New York, and Washington, D.C., and some were formerly enslaved (or children of formerly enslaved parents and grandparents) who became highly successful after the Civil War in a wide range of occupations including working as clergy, politicians, caterers, merchants, and teachers.

The Christmas season was an especially busy time of year for the Black upper class, with numerous dances, balls, and cotillions sponsored by exclusive social clubs, as well as "at homes" and receptions that were held in private residences. Social events in Baltimore and Philadelphia were particularly abundant and lavish. They often included out of town guests, who were honored at teas, luncheons, and receptions during the Christmas season.

Social clubs, which typically ranged in size from one or two dozen to several hundred people, were a huge driver of this circle of activity. Their membership was typically restrictive and included only those whose "behavior and lifestyle conformed to the genteel performance," notes Willard B. Gatewood in his book *Aristocrats of Color*. These included gentlemen's organizations such as the Manhattan (with membership limited to three hundred) and Acanthus Clubs (named after a plant that flourished on the east coast of Africa) in Washington and social groups such as Pittsburgh's Loendi Club (whose members held professional and white-collar jobs) and the Home Social Club of Albany, New York (with a membership of just twelve). The Home Social Club was particularly well known for its yearly Christmas dinner dance, which it hosted for members, their families, and invited guests from out of town.

Another social club that was famous for its annual Christmas balls was the Crescent Club in Philadelphia, the city's leading Black social organization during the Gilded Age. This event included all of the city's "first families" as well as invitees from Washington and New York. In a newspaper account from 1901, the twelfth annual Crescent Club Christmas Ball was given at the "handsome rooms of the club in the Jackson building . . . and at the end of the season it will probably be considered the most brilliant and enjoyable affair of the winter. The evening is spent in music, pleasure and laughter. Stately and handsomely-gowned matrons observe the fleeting scene, dainty maids blush and smile, and in graceful poses, recall an assembly of delicate water color girls." Feathery palms decorated the ballroom, where the Turner-Hallowell orchestra played. The hall and billiard rooms served as a place for young people to meet and flirt, taking a break between dances. A dainty collation featuring a luscious champagne punch was served. "The evening was in every way delightful and a success."

LYNDHURST MANSION, TARRYTOWN, NY

Lemon Drops

Also known as kisses, meringues were a popular Gilded Age holiday treat that incorporated many different flavorings, including lemon, rosewater, vanilla, coconut, and even caraway seeds, creating a large number of taste combinations. Dimples were meringues scattered with crushed almonds. In 1892 an article titled "Christmas Sweet Dishes" in The Girl's Own Paper *claimed that "everyone likes meringues, so be sure and have a heaped dish of them; they are not troublesome nor expensive to make." I agree! This recipe is quite simple; it just requires a kitchen that is not too humid and some time to dry bake the cookies at a low heat.*

MAKES 4½ DOZEN COOKIES

4 egg whites
1 cup superfine sugar*
1 teaspoon lemon juice
2 teaspoons finely grated lemon zest
2 teaspoons cornstarch

Preheat oven to 225°F. Line baking sheets with parchment paper.

Using an electric mixer, beat the egg whites in a large glass or stainless steel bowl on low speed until soft peaks form, about 3–4 minutes, then increase speed to medium and slowly add the sugar a little at a time.

Continue beating until stiff peaks form. Add the lemon juice and rind and beat for about 30 seconds or until well mixed. Add the cornstarch and beat another 30 seconds, just until incorporated.

Using a fork or small cookie scoop, drop meringue about an inch apart on baking sheets, twirling into a "kiss" shape, being careful not to overcrowd. You can also place the meringue in a pastry bag and pipe it onto the baking sheets in a star pattern.

Bake for 1½ hours, rotating once. The time will vary depending on the room temperature and humidity. The cookies will be done when smooth and hard to the touch.

Remove from the oven and allow to cool on the baking sheets for 15 minutes, then transfer to wire racks and let cool completely.

** If you can't find superfine sugar, simply process granulated sugar for one minute in a food processor or blender.*

◀ *Bonbon assortment.* BONBONS COURTESY OF SHANE CONFECTIONERY, PHILADELPHIA, PA

Raisin Penuche

Sometimes called brown sugar fudge, this delicious candy could be found in many iterations during the Gilded Age, often with fruit or nuts, including peanuts, walnuts, pecans, figs, and coconut. A Norwich (CT) Bulletin *article from December 3, 1910, highlights penuche as a "good candy recipe very nice for Christmas," alongside confections such as chocolate caramels, stuffed dates, chocolate fudge, walnut creams, and crackajack (the popcorn and peanut treat we know as Crackerjack). It also suggests making a two-layer fudge using a layer of penuche and one of chocolate fudge. Yum! The recipe here is from my grandmother's mother, Henrietta Ingram Finger (see photo on page 116).*

MAKES ABOUT 1 DOZEN CANDIES

1 cup light brown sugar, packed
½ cup milk
1 tablespoon unsalted butter
¾ cup raisins

Cover a baking sheet with waxed paper. Set aside.

Place brown sugar, milk, and butter in a medium-sized heavy-bottomed pot. Bring to a boil over medium-high heat and continue to boil 8–10 minutes until mixture registers 236°F on a candy thermometer.

Take off burner and cool for 1 minute, then add raisins, stirring until well combined.

Using a small cookie scoop or spoon, drop teaspoon-sized amounts onto waxed paper, leaving about an inch in between.

Set aside to harden. When candies feel dry, remove from waxed paper and store in a tin or plastic container.

Penuche is hailed with acclaim when it appears. . . . [T]he flavor of the candy is improved by sprinkling lightly with salt.

—*FOR THE COMFORT OF THE FAMILY* (1914), BY EMILIE BAKER LORING

Sugar Plums

Dating back to the 1600s, sugar plums started out as small round or oval sweets made out of colored and boiled sugar, similar to what we think of as hard candy today. Related to comfits (sugar-coated seeds), they often had aniseed or caraway seed in the center. By the Gilded Age, they were made from a mixture of chopped dried fruits, nuts, confectioners' sugar, and brandy (which functioned as a flavoring as well as a preservative) and were typically served at the end of the meal with fruit and nuts. They were also sometimes wrapped in colored paper foil and tied up with a ribbon to make a lovely ornament to hang on the Christmas tree.

MAKES ABOUT 4 DOZEN SWEETS

2 cups finely chopped dried figs
2 cups finely chopped pitted dates
2 cups finely chopped dried apricots
2 cups chopped almonds
2 tablespoons brandy
Confectioners' sugar

Mix dried fruits, nuts, and brandy in a large bowl. Slowly add confectioners' sugar until mixture binds together.

Shape into bite-sized balls and then roll in more confectioners' sugar. Store in an airtight container in the refrigerator for up to 2 weeks.

An Idle Fascination with Bonbons

Bonbons—bite-sized, filled chocolate confections—have long been associated with luxury, indulgence, and elaborate celebration, so it is fitting that they would appear on so many menus throughout the Gilded Age. Even the phrase "sitting around eating bonbons," to express idleness, can be traced back to the Gilded Age and its leisure class.

Although the term *bonbon* originated in the French court in the 1600s and first referred to sugar-coated almonds or fruit, the term later came to mean fine, small, bite-sized chocolates, often filled with caramel or fruit gelee, which were first made by specialty French confectionists and imported to the United States for consumption by a very privileged few.

By the mid-1800s, fueled by automation and newer processing techniques, American confectionaries began opening their own candy shops to compete with the quality of imported French chocolates. "The nineteenth-century invention of solid chocolate that could be melted and used to coat sweets before drying to a form a hard shell promoted the proliferation of chocolate truffles with chocolate ganache centers and other small chocolate-covered bonbons," according to *the Oxford Companion to Sugar and Sweets*.

At the beginning of the Gilded Age, bonbons became de rigueur among the wealthy urban social set, a fitting symbol of the luxury associated with French cuisine, couture, and customs. The go-to mid-nineteenth-century dining etiquette guide of the upper classes, *Godey's Lady's Book*, noted that bonbons and fruits should directly follow the dessert course. Bonbons appeared on menus ranging from the famed Delmonico's restaurant in New York in 1888 to a private dinner hosted by the Vanderbilt family in their Fifth Avenue townhouse in 1899.

Perhaps it is no surprise that few cookbooks of the time include recipes to make chocolate candy at home. Recipes for easier to make "Parisian sweets"—figs, dates, and chopped walnuts tossed in confectioners' sugar—can be found in some period cookbooks, and these provided a less costly alternative to expensive store-bought bonbons.

Certainly no Gilded Ager worth her fine crystal and China would serve bonbons made at home. Instead, bonbons were generally considered a luxury import or bought at specialty confectionary stores in big cities. As demand grew for bonbons, so did domestic production. Philadelphia was especially known for its confectioners, with James Parkinson and Stephen Whitman among the over two hundred confectioners who opened small retail shops there. The port city imported sugar from the Caribbean and became a large sugar-refining center, turning many businessmen into "sugar magnates," whose success fueled the construction of a host of large Gilded Age mansions in and around Philadelphia.

Over time, with the introduction of large-scale sugar processing and bulk-production machines, bonbons became more affordable for the middle classes. Whitman first brought the idea of bonbons to the mass market by offering a box of "Choice Mixed Sugar Plums" in 1854: the first packaged confection in a printed, marketed box produced to present as a gift. Whitman's first newspaper ads appeared during the holidays of 1860 and advertised "Chocolate, Bonbons and Confections." It was not until 1912, however, that Whitman introduced the Whitman Sampler box of chocolate that we still know today, according to Russel Stover, which now owns the Whitman brand.

Much like today, bonbons were given as gifts, especially during the holidays, and like so much that happened during the Gilded Age, this was just one more way in which to show off one's wealth and sophistication, as well as affection for the recipient.

Contributed by food historian and culinary stylist Dan Macey

Christmas Games

There were many games associated with Christmas during the Gilded Age, many stemming from English traditions. Snapdragon was a game that could be played on Christmas Eve or Christmas Day after the main meal. Raisins, currants, and other dried fruit were piled on a shallow dish and doused with a liberal amount of brandy. The room was then darkened, and the pile was set on fire. In the glowing light, players were supposed to grab the blazing fruit, blow out any flames, and then eat it—yikes! According to *Christmas: Its Origin and Associations* (1902), "a good deal of merriment was caused by the unsuccessful efforts of competitors for the raisins in the flaming bowl." Both bravery and swiftness were definitely helpful player attributes! There was even a traditional song that went along with the game:

Here he comes with the flaming bowl,
Don't be mean to take his toll,
Snip! Snap! Dragon!

Take care you don't take too much,
Be not greedy in your clutch,
Snip! Snap! Dragon!

With his blue and lapping tongue
Many of you will be stung,
Snip! Snap! Dragon!

For he snaps at all that comes
Snatching at his feast of plums,
Snip! Snap! Dragon!

But Old Christmas makes him come,
Though he looks so fee! fa! fum!
Snip! Snap! Dragon!

Don't 'ee fear him, be but bold—
Out he goes, his flames are cold.
Snip! Snap! Dragon!

Christmas evening was a big occasion for children's parties. For little ones, there was a game called the Christmas Bag, which is very similar to the piñatas sometimes featured at children's birthday parties today. For this game, a large white or silver paper bag was filled with sugar plums and/or small toys and tied with a string, then suspended from the ceiling or a large door frame. Each player was then blindfolded and given three tries to hit the bag with a light stick, tearing it open and thus scattering the treats for all to retrieve and enjoy.

LYNDHURST MANSION, TARRYTOWN, NY

Popcorn Balls

Candy stores throughout the Gilded Age advertised popcorn balls as a perfect stocking stuffer for children during the holidays. Some confectioners sold the treats directly to customers for a penny while others also advertised them for wholesale purchase, often to young peddlers, called "candy boys." While the balls were sold in stores, they could also be made at home. An early recipe for popcorn balls appeared in an 1861 cookbook by E. F. Haskell titled The Housekeeper's Encyclopedia of Cooking and Domestic Economy, *a popular guide for novice housewives. The recipe called for boiling "honey, maple or other sugar to the great thread," a reference to the soft ball stage, about 230°F. The inexpensive treat was especially popular in the South because sorghum syrup and corn were both easily found there right after the Civil War, while other cooking ingredients were still scarce. Here's an updated recipe that doesn't involve bringing the sugar mixture to high heat and adds marshmallows to help bind the popcorn.*

MAKES 20 BALLS

20 cups of popped corn (homemade is best, using about ¾ cup raw kernels)
¾ cup light corn syrup
½ stick (4 tablespoons) unsalted butter
2 teaspoons cold water
2 cups confectioners' sugar
1 cup well-packed mini marshmallows
1 teaspoon vanilla
1 teaspoon salt

Line a baking sheet with parchment or waxed paper and set aside.

Place the popped corn in a large bowl.

In a medium saucepan, over medium-high heat, combine the corn syrup, butter, water, confectioners' sugar, and marshmallows. Heat and stir until well combined and the mixture comes to a boil. Allow to cook for several more minutes. Remove from the heat and add in the vanilla and salt.

Pour the liquid mixture over the popcorn and toss with a wooden spoon until the popcorn is thoroughly coated.

Let the popcorn cool slightly until you can handle the mixture with your hands. Then with greased hands, quickly form the popcorn mixture into 3-inch balls and place them on the lined baking sheets to cool completely.

Eat immediately or wrap in plastic wrap and serve later; you can even freeze them.

Popcorn Balls

CONTINUED

ADDITIONAL TIPS

- Feel free to add several drops of food coloring to the sugar mixture if you would like to produce more festive, colored balls. Or add 2 tablespoons of sprinkles when you toss the syrup mixture with the popcorn, for added holiday flair.
- Be sure to grease your hands with cooking spray or butter when forming the balls.
- Work quickly, because as the mixture cools down, the balls get harder to shape. It's a great activity to get the family to help.
- Don't form them too tightly: press firmly enough to shape but not too tight that they will be tough to chew.
- Feel free to embed a wire hook into the top of the ball when forming it to allow it to be used as an ornament.

Contributed by food historian and culinary stylist Dan Macey

Christmas Parties

During the Gilded Age, Broadway and Fifth Avenue in New York City was home to a number of large, elegant hotels such as the Waldorf, Plaza, St. Regis, Astor, and Knickerbocker. All of these featured private dining rooms, and many wealthy families liked to host Christmas dinner parties in these lavish settings, which were decked out with an abundance of mistletoe, holly, and other winter greenery; brightly ornamented Christmas trees; colorful flowers; and lush potted plants. The holiday theme also included decorations made out of confectionary, such as the candy Santa Claus souvenirs and replica of the Hotel Knickerbocker the hotel's chef crafted in 1908.

These private dining rooms in places like the Waldorf-Astoria were often filled to capacity, many times by out-of-state families who had children attending New York boarding schools or universities. These parties included the families of industry men such as L. G. Kaufmann, a Michigan lumber company executive; politicians such as New Jersey senator Frank O. Briggs; military leaders such as Captain Tillinghast L'Hommedieu Huston (who later co-owned the New York Yankees); and musical celebrities such as tenor Enrico Caruso. Other celebrations included evening entertainment for the little ones, such as magicians, Punch and Judy shows, and vaudeville acts. Food included delicacies such as roast pig, turkey, and salmon and huge bowls of eggnog decorated with fruit and holly.

Christmas parties given at private homes were another celebratory option for the well-to-do. One particularly unique party, held on December 25, 1889, was actually also a surprise party for Caroline Astor, the American socialite who (along with fellow social climber Ward McAllister) presided over the exclusive Four Hundred, the elite list of the only people the two society ringleaders deemed socially worthy. The idea was conceived by Cornelia Bradley-Martin (wife of socialite Bradley Martin), who was able to distract Caroline at her house on 22 West 20th Street while the festivities were being prepared. The two ladies (decked out in white satin trimmed with holly) then arrived at Mrs. Astor's home on Fifth Avenue to an elaborately decorated ballroom. Copious amounts of holly branches and snowballs made from white carnations and white violets were prominently displayed throughout the ballroom, and a gigantic Santa Claus was tucked into the alcove between the ballroom and dining room. Two rows of small silk and satin stockings in various hues filled with toys and bonbons (meant to be party favors for the guests) were stretched across the ebony fireplace, and a large bough of mistletoe hung from the balcony. There were thirty-six couples in total, many from families well-known to the Gilded Age roster, with surnames such as Roosevelt, Vanderbilt, Dyer, and Goelet. Henry Le Grand Cannon (an artist and collector whose family owned Lake Champlain Transportation in Vermont) played Santa Claus, pushing a sleigh decorated with smilax and holly and tied with red, green, and yellow ribbons and filled with miniature Santa Clauses, dolls, and other toys around the ballroom, distributing gifts to the guests.

Doughnut Hole Croquembouche

SERVES 10–12

1 5 × 18-inch Styrofoam cone from a hobby shop

1 cake stand

1 tub of vanilla frosting (such as Pillsbury or Betty Crocker)

12 dozen glazed doughnut holes

A box of toothpicks

1 bag cranberries

1 bunch fresh rosemary

Confectioners' sugar and a small sifter

Secure the cone to the cake stand with cake icing.

Begin at the bottom and secure the doughnut holes to the cone using the toothpicks. Make sure your doughnut holes are snug together so that the cone doesn't show through. Continue covering the cone to the top.

Garnish the tree with the cranberries, using the toothpicks. Stick sprigs of rosemary in between some of the holes. Then liberally sprinkle the entire tree with confectioners' sugar.

Recipe contributed by food historian and culinary stylist Dan Macey

Piéce Montée: Glittering Centerpieces of the Gilded Age

Gilded Age hostesses were known for entertaining on a large and lavish scale. And when it came to the centerpiece for a fancy dinner table, ball, or holiday celebration, extravagance was the name of the game. Chefs and designers were hired to create *piéces montées* (pronounced pees maan-tee), large, decorative architectural or sculptural creations made from confectionary materials, such as almond paste, nougat, spun sugar, and pastillage, a natural binding agent made from long-lasting sugar paste mixed with moistened gum.

Piéce montée is French, literally meaning "assembled piece" or "mounted piece." The pieces were often made to resemble classic architecture, such as Roman temples or Egyptian pyramids, or fancy inspirations from nature such as floral landscapes or animal scenes. The pastillage-made centerpieces could be kept almost indefinitely when stored in a dry place and were often reused. The paste could be colored, rolled, shaped, and then left to dry before assembling into astonishing creations towering as high as five feet. While they were edible, their main purpose was to serve as a stunning and breathtaking centerpiece.

Elaborate centerpieces made from sugar had appeared on the tables of European nobility during the early seventeenth century. Creating these centerpieces "was a time-consuming specialty, a skill that demanded technical and creative abilities," according to food historian Anne Willan, in *The Edible Monument: The Art of Food for Festivals.* "Italian confectioners were the masters of the towering sugar sculptures called *trionfi*, and were intermingled with food," Willan added. One guest at a royal dinner noted that "their use as entertainment, is to gratify the eye, as the meat, music and perfumes do the other senses."

The Gilded Age chefs revived these flamboyant centerpieces with the addition of newer cooking techniques and additional stabilizing ingredients such as glycerin, gelatin, and liquid glucose.

One of the largest *piéces montées* displayed during the Gilded Age was created on the occasion of the centennial of the inauguration of George Washington at a ball thrown at the Metropolitan Opera House in New York in 1899. In what was called "decorations on a scale of lavish magnificence" by the *Evening World* newspaper, 132 *piéces montées* were on display at a 550-foot buffet table. Chef Eugene Laperruque of the Hoffman House "reigned supreme, exhibiting some of the choicest creations of art," according to the newspaper account. Laperruque had been the chef at Delmonico's restaurants and for the famed Rothschild family in New York.

Piéces montées were not just constructed for the New York elite. Chef J. D. Kueney of the Stag restaurant in Cincinnati drew thousands to his restaurants for New Year's Eve to witness his *piéces montées*, made not just from confectionery ingredients but wild game. "The Battle of Yellowstone Park" was described as "the most attractive," according to the *Cincinnati Enquirer* in 1899. "A bear has killed an elk and holds the victim beneath his paw. A savage wolf is approaching to contest and fight for the meal, and the bear is turning upon him with bold defiance," is how the piece was described. And there is more. "Above the stirring scene are grouped gold and silver pheasants, rabbits and animals." And even more amazing, according to the newspaper, "is that every animal has been cooked first, then posed and covered with his rightful skin . . . and then eaten by guests at the New Year's reception."

While most of the *piéces montées* at the lavish events were created by professional chefs, *Ladies Home Journal* magazine, toward the end of the Gilded Age, was advising housewives how to create their own impressive centerpieces at home, especially for the holidays. For one Christmas centerpiece the magazine asked housewives to "select a smooth block of ice weighing 30 pounds." Then "with a sharp chisel hollow out a receptacle for grapes, white and purple." The magazine then recommended presenting the piece on a silver tray lined with absorbent cotton and decorating the sides with additional grapes and grape leaves. Of course, finding a large block of ice was much easier then, and it could probably be acquired by simply asking the ice man for an additional block when he came to deliver ice for early versions of home refrigerators, which were cooled with ice blocks stored in insulated metal compartments.

Piéce montée now has come to refer to an edible dessert known as croquembouche, an assemblage—usually stacked into a tall cone space—made from choux pastry profiteroles or cream puffs. Amber-colored spun sugar is often wrapped around the structure for added pizazz.

In a nod to the Gilded Age's lavish holiday centerpieces, we devised an easier, but equally impressive, croquembouche using store-bought glazed doughnut holes and some items from the craft store. This is perfect for a holiday dessert or for serving while opening presents.

Contributed by food historian and culinary stylist Dan Macey

Hot Chocolate

Even though we often use hot chocolate *and* hot cocoa *interchangeably today, during the Gilded Age they were two distinctly different beverages. Hot chocolate was thicker and almost syrupy, made by grating fine-quality chocolate and pouring it over boiling water to dissolve. Then fresh milk, sugar, and sometimes egg yolks were added. Hot cocoa was lighter in color and intensity, made from grated cocoa beans boiled with milk and water, without the addition of eggs and sugar. As you can imagine, hot chocolate was the reigning chocolate beverage of the two options. Thick, rich, and immensely satisfying, it was an intense and stimulating drink widely served at tea parties, receptions, and kettledrums (informal afternoon or early evening social parties featuring a light meal). In the early 1900s, soda fountains often referred to hot chocolate as "Christmas Cheer" and recommended that a cup of this warming drink could remove "that tired feeling from shopping."*

2 ounces (½ package) unsweetened baking chocolate
1¼ cups milk (preferably 2% or whole)
2 tablespoons sugar (or to taste)

Place a mixing bowl and beaters in the freezer for about 15 minutes.

Place the chocolate in a microwave-safe dish and heat in the microwave on high for 30 seconds. Take out the dish and give the chocolate a stir. Continue doing this in 30-second intervals until chocolate is melted. Set aside.

Heat the milk in a small saucepan over medium heat until small bubbles begin to form around the edges, about 2–3 minutes. Turn heat to low and add the chocolate and sugar. Increase heat to medium-low and stir with a whisk until smooth and slightly thickened. Pour into a mug and allow to cool slightly. Mixture will thicken upon standing, so give it a good stir and/or add more milk in small increments until preferred consistency. Top with fresh whipped cream if desired.

◀ *Bonbon assortment.* COURTESY OF SHANE CONFECTIONERY, PHILADELPHIA, PA

Hot Chocolate

CONTINUED

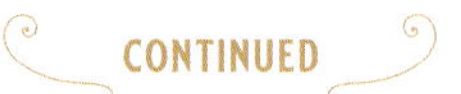

FOR THE WHIPPED CREAM

1 cup heavy cream

2 tablespoons confectioners' sugar

½ teaspoon vanilla

Remove the mixing bowl and beaters from the freezer. Add the heavy cream, confectioners' sugar, and vanilla to the bowl and whip using an electric mixer on medium speed for about 5 minutes or until firm peaks form.

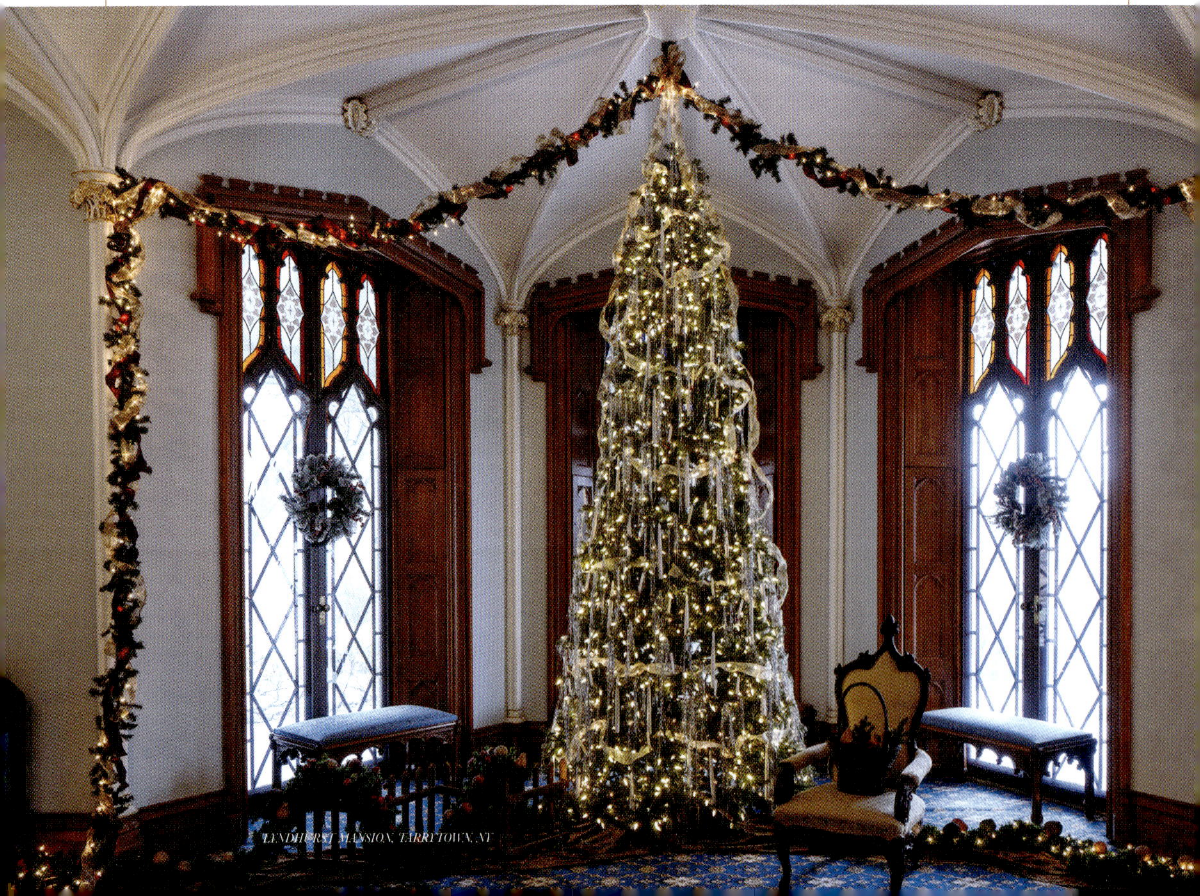

LYNDHURST MANSION, TARRYTOWN, NY

Mustache Cup

The Gilded Age was a time of extravagance, including the trend toward long, luxuriant mustaches. So what were men who sported one of these flourishing facial accessories supposed to do if they wanted to drink a cup of hot tea, coffee, or chocolate? Well there was an answer to that: mustache cups! These special cups had a ledge to guard and keep mustaches dry while men sipped their favorite drink.

Turns out they were also popular Christmas presents in the Gilded Age for husbands, beaus, and fathers, alongside other "masculine" gifts such as silk ties, slippers, shaving mugs, and fountain pens. They also served as the subject of satirical jests regarding the lack of facial hair some men were unable to grow. For example, an item in the December 1881 issue of Lehigh University's student publication *The Lehigh Burr* stated, "One of the sophomores lately received a mustache cup as a birthday present. His friends maliciously suggest that perhaps Santa Claus will take pity on him and send along a mustache as a Christmas gift."

Christmas Shopping

Even back in the Gilded Age, newspapers and magazines (the media of the day) recommended shopping early to avoid "the jam of late bundle-laden buyers that usually pushes its way through the stores a week or ten days before Christmas." They also suggested shopping in the morning versus the afternoon, such as depicted in this verse from a poem by W. J. Lampton that ran in a December 1908 *New York Times*:

Do your shopping in the morning,
That's the early Christmas warning;
Thus it is you miss the rushing,
Crowding, jamming, shoving, crushing,
Kicking, scrapping, swearing, growling,
Slamming, slapping, banging, scowling,
Waiting, tiring, sweating, mopping
Incident to Christmas shopping.

Also like today, many publications provided shopping tips and gift ideas (typically based on the papers' advertisers). A December 1878 *Philadelphia Inquirer* article raved about the festive décor throughout the city, stating that "every shop is a sort of universal exposition of all that is beautiful or attractive," and "streets and shops are crowded with purchasers of gifts." The article goes on to comment on the rivalry among shop merchants, with each trying to outdo each other in terms of the size and attractiveness of their holiday displays and gift offerings. But this article claimed the best way to save time, trouble, and money before heading out "on a Christmas shopping expedition" was to look through the paper's advertising columns and make a list of stores to visit. Even then, advertising was the way to bring in Christmas shoppers. As further noted in the article, "People at this season are so busy, there is so much to do and so little time in which to do it, that they go at once to the stores of those who advertise the sorts and varieties of the goods they sell."

But for those who wanted to avoid the fast-paced hustle and bustle of holiday shopping, a new alternative entered the scene during the Gilded Age: catalog shopping. Merchants touted the ease and convenience of this new shopping method. In 1872 retailer Montgomery Ward started its mail-order catalog business; Sears, Roebuck and Company followed a bit later in 1886. By the 1890s, Montgomery Ward

Christmas shoppers on Sixth Avenue, New York City, early 1900s.
NEW YORK PUBLIC LIBRARY DIGITAL COLLECTIONS, WALLACH DIVISION PICTURE COLLECTION

called its catalog the Great Wish Book, with Sears producing an even bigger catalog in 1897, which weighed in at a whopping 786 pages of merchandise. Even smaller, more specialized retailers got into the act. Loftis Diamond Cutters, Watchmakers and Jewelers of Chicago ran an ad in a December 1905 *Keith's Magazine on Home Building* with the huge headline "Christmas Diamonds on Credit," urging shoppers to "select from our Handsome Catalogue the articles you desire, and we will send them to you for examination and approval. If satisfactory, retain them, paying one-fifth the cost and the balance in eight equal monthly payments; if not, return to us." Loftis further stated the company would take all risks and pay all express charges. What a bargain!

Abram S. Isaacs, American rabbi, author, and professor.
WIKIMEDIA COMMONS

Nineteenth-century Hanukkah lamp.
WIKIMEDIA COMMONS

Chapter Five
HANUKKAH

We Hebrews disguise it as we may, cannot but feel the genial influence of the Christmastide.
DR. ABRAM S. ISAACS, *JEWISH MESSENGER*, 1889

THE GILDED AGE was a time when Hanukkah celebrations in America began to become more prevalent and widespread among the Jewish community, alongside the growth of more festive and commercial Christmas celebrations. Seeing Christians celebrate Christmas, many Jewish families also wanted to partake of some December merriment. Since Hanukkah occurs around the same time of year, it was a natural fit. "We share their larger meaning and bless the genial men and women who through Christmas bounty cheer and brighten mankind," said Dr. Abram S. Isaacs in an 1889 issue of *Jewish Messenger*. In terms of holiday presents, the Jewish tradition of giving gelt (money) to the needy and giving some to children (with the thought that they would pass it on and learn about charitable giving) aligned with the Christmas gift-giving tradition.

Although there were no specific foods associated with Hanukkah when the holiday first originated and "the Maccabees and the generations that followed had never heard of latkes and *sufganiyot* (a small, deep-fried doughnut), they did know how to spread out a feast," note Lori Stein and Ronald H. Isaacs in *Let's Eat: Jewish Food and Faith*. And since a meal was often capped off with a sweet treat, there may have been desserts in the form of small doughy cakes, similar to Greek *loukomades* (leavened and deep-fried dough balls soaked in syrup or honey). These delicacies were the forerunners to *sufganiyots* and among the earliest type of sweets people ate.

Fried doughnuts in all kinds of variations are common in Jewish cuisine throughout the world, with *sufganiyots* most associated with Hanukkah. It is commonly thought the term has its origins in the word *Sufan* (meaning Greek for spongy), typically describing a type of jelly doughnut. And the tradition of sweetening and frying dough is even older and more widespread. By the beginning of the twentieth century, *Berliners* (fried doughnuts filled with jelly) were a popular New Year's Eve dessert in Eastern Europe; in Poland, *ponchki* were a similar treat.

In the late nineteenth century, Jewish immigrants brought latkes (potato pancakes) to America, a Hanukkah dish favored by those of Eastern European descent. They were fried in oil, symbolizing the small amount of oil that miraculously lasted for eight days when the Maccabees rededicated the ancient Temple in Jerusalem. By 1903, advertisements in Yiddish American newspapers marketed food gifts such as fruit as an accompaniment to Hanukkah latkes, along with tea and coffee to round out the celebratory meal. And at Hanukkah festivities held by Jewish congregations in Gilded Age America, children were often treated to ice cream.

Jelly Doughnuts for Hanukkah

During the Gilded Age, serving jelly doughnuts and potato latkes fried in oil became part of Jewish household Hanukkah celebrations. Consuming food fried in oil at Hanukkah commemorates the miracle associated with the Temple oil. The story relates that after the Maccabees, a small Jewish army, secured the Temple in Jerusalem from the Greeks, they needed to rededicate it by lighting the Temple with purified oil. Although they only had enough oil to last one night, miraculously, the oil lasted for eight nights. Thus, the genesis of the Hanukkah tradition of lighting the menorah for eight nights. The first American Jewish cookbook, Jewish Cookery Book, *by Esther Levy, was published in Philadelphia in 1871. It contains two recipes for "dough nuts," one of which we have modernized below. These doughnuts were popularized first in Poland, where they were fried in chicken fat rather than lard, following kosher laws.*

MAKES ABOUT 20 DOUGHNUTS

1 packet dry active yeast (2¼ teaspoons)
1 cup warm water
3 tablespoons sugar
3 cups flour
½ teaspoon salt
1 egg
1½ tablespoons vegetable oil
½ teaspoon ground nutmeg
Zest of 1 lemon
1 tablespoon orange liqueur
Vegetable oil for frying
1 cup confectioners' sugar
2 cups strawberry jam

Combine the yeast, warm water, and sugar in a small bowl and stir. Allow the yeast to activate and expand and get foamy, which should take about 10 minutes. (If it doesn't, your yeast has expired and you should throw it out.)

Meanwhile, combine the flour, salt, egg, vegetable oil, nutmeg, lemon zest, and orange liqueur in a large bowl. Once the yeast has activated, add it to the bowl and mix with a spatula until a sticky dough forms.

Remove the dough onto a well-floured surface and knead for about 8 minutes until dough is smooth and soft and bounces back when poked with a finger. You may need to add additional flour to prevent sticking.

Jelly Doughnuts for Hanukkah

CONTINUED

Place the dough in a well-oiled bowl and cover with a tea towel, then place in a warm place and allow to rise until doubled, about 1–2 hours.

Remove the dough from the bowl and roll out onto a well-floured surface to about ¼ inch thickness. Using a biscuit cutter, cookie cutter, or glass, cut into 2½-inch rounds. Gather up the scraps from the cutting and re-roll them out to cut out additional doughnuts. Place on a well-floured baking sheet, cover with plastic wrap, and allow to rise for another 15 minutes.

Heat the oil to 325°F.

In small batches, using a slotted spoon, carefully slip 2–3 rounds into oil. (A small fryer is perfect for this.) Fry until golden on one side, about 40 seconds, then flip over the dough and fry the other side for another 40 seconds. Using a slotted spoon, transfer the doughnuts to a paper-towel-lined baking sheet. Sprinkle with confectioners' sugar and allow to cool slightly.

With a small knife, make a hole in the top of each doughnut. Fill a piping bag or squirt bottle with the jam. Fill each doughnut with the jam through the hole you just made. Allow some of the jam to ooze out to form a dot on the center of the doughnut.

The doughnuts are best when eaten soon after you make them or later that day.

Contributed by food historian and culinary stylist Dan Macey

Hanukkah in the Gilded Age

Celebrating Hanukkah, the Festival of Lights, grew in popularity for American Jews during the Gilded Age. A group of Jewish leaders used Hanukkah to unify the various ethnic and religious groups immigrating into the United States. And while Hanukkah had been celebrated for centuries, the Gilded Age marked a greater visibility for Jewish culture and religion in American society.

Hanukkah is the eight-day Jewish celebration that falls at the end of the year and commemorates the rededication of a Jerusalem temple after a group of Jewish fighters, known as the Maccabees, defeated the Greek Syrians in the second century BC. The word *Hanukkah* is Hebrew for dedication and can be spelled Chanukkah or Hanukkah. Each of the eight nights of Hanukkah, a candle is lit on a ceremonial candelabra called a menorah to commemorate the story of the Maccabees, for whom one day's worth of oil lasted for eight days.

Hanukkah became one way that religious leaders helped unify the Jewish immigrants, by using the holiday, with its themes of religious freedom and light, to become a symbol of Jewish resilience and assimilation into American society. The holiday served as a way for Jews to maintain their identities amid the greater American Christian population, who were experiencing the transformation of Christmas from a religious observance to a more secular American holiday.

"Hanukkah emerged as a newly meaningful holiday for nineteenth-century American Jewish leaders because its story provided images and lessons useful to clergy and lay leaders on all sides of a heated debate about how Judaism should adapt to America," according to Dianne Ashton in her book *Hanukkah in America*. Newspapers at the time often referred to Hanukkah as "Jewish Christmas"; although that wasn't accurate, many Jewish leaders didn't object to the reference since it began to explain the holiday to Christians.

As waves of new Jewish immigrants arrived in America, and especially in New York's Lower East Side, "less emphasis was placed on the holiday's religious reform and more on gift giving and other forms of pleasure," according to *Savoring Gotham, a Food Lover's Companion to New York City*.

American Jewish leaders primarily focused Hanukkah festivities on children as a way to counter Christmas, which was also becoming a celebration centered around the family and children. The tradition of giving children Hanukkah gelt, usually coins, became more popular and a way to teach gratitude, as the children often gave the money to their teachers or religious leaders. The tradition of giving gold-foil-covered chocolate gelt did not begin until the 1920s, when a New York–based candy company took advantage of the increasing popularity of Hanukkah.

Food associated with Hanukkah includes potato pancakes or latkes, which are fried in oil to symbolize the Maccabee's oil, which miraculously lasted eight days. Potato pancake recipes were brought by Eastern European Jews, who often used *schmaltz*—chicken, duck, or geese fat—to cook the potatoes. In the early twentieth century, Crisco, the first entirely vegetable oil product, was sold in an advertising campaign targeted toward kosher-keeping Jews. "Crisco, the first brand of shortening to be made entirely of vegetable oil, happened to be neither dairy nor meat, making it the perfect product to hawk to Yiddish speaking immigrant mothers, and their more assimilated daughters wanting to cook with more advanced, processed American items like Crisco," noted Shira Feder in a 2018 article in *Forward*, an independent national Jewish newspaper.

Another popular Hanukkah recipe, also cooked in oil, is for jelly doughnuts, or *sufganiyot*, coming from the Greek word for puffed and fried (see recipe on page 140).

In 1871 the first Jewish cookbook was published in America, *Jewish Cookery Book*. Its author, Esther Jacobs Levy, was from Philadelphia and combined recipes from different Jewish backgrounds—English, German, Sephardic, and American—and addressed how to cook like a Jewish American. "Having undertaken the present work with the view of proving that, without violating the precepts of our religion, a table can be spread which will satisfy the appetites of the most fastidious," Levy wrote in her *Jewish Cookery Book*. She even suggested that the main Sabbath meal take place on Sunday, instead of the more traditional Saturday holy day, to accommodate the Jewish merchant class. "When husbands are at home, then something good must be prepared in honor of the lords of the household," Levy advised.

"German cuisine was the first to influence the mainstream of American-Jewish life, with about 150,000 German Jews having settled in the country by the time of the Civil War," says noted Jewish cookbook author Joan Nathan. As more Jews immigrated to the United States, from a wider array of countries and varying degrees of religious observance, conflicts arose with regard to maintaining a kosher household.

But Jews, even wealthy bankers and owners of large department stores, were still not allowed to join most big city social clubs and were not invited to lavish Gilded Age holiday parties that took place at the elite Four Hundred's mansions. "Not a single Jew could boast of an invitation to any of the houses of the Four Hundred," wrote Elizabeth Drexel Lehr, a member of the Four Hundred, in her tell-all book *King Lear and the Gilded Age*, published in 1935. "They could give them lunches in restaurants, take them to the theatre if they chose, but they must not bring them home," she noted.

That was until James Speyers, the first Jewish person to be accepted into the Four Hundred. His fiancée at the time, Ellen Dynley Prince, had opened a tearoom in New York that was very popular with the elite, including Mrs. Astor, Mrs. Oelrichs, and Mrs. Cornelius Vanderbilt. Miss Prince called on Mrs. Astor, the leader of the Four Hundred, and asked her advice on marrying Speyers. After much consideration, Mrs. Astor responded, according to Elizabeth Lehr's book, "I don't think we have any alternative, for we are all so fond of you. Marry him, my dear, if you want to. I for one will invite you both to my parties, and I think everyone else will do the same." And most of them did.

Contributed by food historian and culinary stylist Dan Macey

LYNDHURST MANSION, TARRYTOWN, NY

Chapter Six
New Year's Desserts

On New Year's Day, friends, old and young, called to wish each other a Happy New Year. Everybody was welcome, even strangers, and there were crullers and New Year's cakes and all kinds of good things to eat and drink.
A HOME GEOGRAPHY OF NEW YORK CITY, 1905

Many New Year's desserts were seasonal treats brought to America by Dutch settlers during colonial times, particularly the New York region. New Year's cookies (sometimes called New Year's cakes) were sweet delicacies typically flavored with caraway seeds, lemon, and sometimes apple cider or nutmeg. They were handed out to visitors during New Year's calling (open house) celebrations, common among New Yorkers in the nineteenth century.

The shapes of New Year's cookies could vary depending on the cookie cutters available in each household, but geometric shapes like circles, rectangles, and diamonds were popular. Another method for making these cookies called for pressing the dough into carved wooden molds, decorated with shapes ranging from floral and animal patterns to famous people and characters such as George Washington and Rip Van Winkle, to create an embossed cookie, similar to German springerle cookies. A third technique, described in a cookbook from 1883, says New Year's cookies were originally made in large thin cakes (the size of a dinner plate) and freshly cut into pieces to serve to each guest as they arrived. Although they peaked in popularity in the mid-nineteenth century, recipes for New Year's cookies can still be found in cookbooks throughout the Gilded Age, sometimes referred to as New York cookies.

As the New Year's calling custom started to fall out of favor toward the end of the nineteenth century, New Year's parties (held in either private homes or hotels and restaurants) became more popular, featuring some of the same desserts served at Christmas, such as plum pudding and mince and pumpkin pies, as well as coconut custard pie; lady fingers; coffee mousse; macaroons; biscuit glacé (a rich custardy dessert made with sponge cake and vanilla liquor); ice cream with flavors such as ginger, vanilla, and coffee; fruit and nuts; bonbons; cheese and crackers; and café noir (black coffee). Specialty cakes were often made in novel shapes, such as the Roman god Janus (who symbolized both beginnings and endings) depicted with two faces: an older face looking backward and a younger face looking forward, representing the old and new years.

LYNDHURST MANSION, TARRYTOWN, NY

A 1905 *Good Housekeeping* article describes a supper table for a New Year's party as being decked out with holly and bright red candles. Red ribbons were looped from the center to each place setting, which featured red carnations for the women and boxes of chocolate cigarettes for the men. One of the women's place settings also had a few sprays of mignonette (a plant with white or yellow spiky flowers), and one of the men's place settings had a boutonniere of white narcissus. Both were hidden from view under the ribbon, with the idea that those who happened to choose the places with these favors would "marry before the year's end."

New Year's Cookies

Not overly sweet, these cookies have a warm and slightly spicy flavor due to the inclusion of caraway seeds, which are often used to flavor bread. But caraway (known for freshening the breath) was also an ingredient in sweet baked goods during the Christmas season, including sugar plums, comfits (candies made from seeds or nuts coated in several layers of sugar), as well as small cakes and cookies. These cookies are very pretty cut in the shapes of diamonds and hearts.

MAKES ABOUT 3 DOZEN COOKIES

1 stick (½ cup) unsalted butter, softened
1 cup sugar
2 eggs
2¾ cups all-purpose flour
1 teaspoon baking powder
1 teaspoon cream of tartar
¼ teaspoon salt
2 teaspoons caraway seeds
1 teaspoon lemon zest

Preheat oven to 350°F. Line baking sheets with parchment paper.

Using an electric mixer, cream the butter and sugar together in a bowl, then beat in the eggs.

Sift the flour, baking powder, cream of tartar, and salt together in a separate bowl, then slowly add to the wet ingredients. Stir in the caraway seeds and lemon zest and continue to mix until combined. If dough seems sticky, add up to ½ cup additional flour in small increments until dough is easy to handle.

Roll out the dough on a floured surface to a thickness of a little more than ¼ inch and cut into heart, diamond, and rectangular shapes. Place on baking sheets about 2 inches apart and prick all over with a fork.

Bake for 10–12 minutes. Remove from the oven and sprinkle tops with granulated sugar. Cool for a few minutes and then transfer to wire racks to cool completely.

New Year's Calling

New Year's calling was a social ritual dating back to the Dutch settlers who came to the New York area in the seventeenth century. They welcomed the new year by opening their houses to family and friends on January 1. It was considered a breach of etiquette to leave out any acquaintances, and even strangers with "presentable appearances" were typically welcomed. Gentlemen used the day to make social calls for the purpose of wishing each other health and happiness, renewing friendships, or repairing troubled relationships. Ladies stayed at home and offered New Year's cakes and other cookies, flavored with signature Dutch flavorings of caraway, coriander, cardamom, and honey, as well as more substantial dishes such as truffled fowl (poultry stuffed with truffles), oysters à la poulette (oysters in a cream sauce), and fruitcake, often paired with refreshments such as cherry bounce (a type of cordial), sherry, Madeira wine, eggnog, and hot punch.

By the early nineteenth century, this custom of "visiting and feasting" was a tradition practiced by all New Yorkers, including many old upper-class Black families. Women hosted these open houses, and men did the socializing, making their way from one house to another, enjoying the abundant food and drinks offered at each home. Since it was a day celebrated with such tremendous eating and drinking, things could sometimes get a bit riotous and out of hand. According to *Curiosities of Popular Customs and of Rites, Ceremonies, Observances and Miscellaneous Antiquities* (1898), "Young men in barouches (carriages) would rattle from one house to another all day long. . . . There was a noisy and hilarious greeting, a glass of wine was swallowed hurriedly, everybody shook hands all around, and the callers dashed out and rushed into the carriage and were driven rapidly to the next house."

The New Year's calling ritual extended into other regions around the United States, with each area putting their own spin on the custom, such as depicted in the *Kansas Home Cook-Book* (1886), which suggested consulting expected gentlemen callers beforehand since "they prefer rather substantial dishes." Recommended food included hot coffee, tea, chocolate, and bouillon; sandwiches; salads; pickles; jellies; three or four kinds of cold meats; scalloped oysters; ornamental cakes for decoration; one or two baskets of mixed cake; and fresh fruits such as bananas, oranges, and white grapes. This book advises not serving wine, deeming it "dangerous" to partake of different varietals at each home and also potentially getting overheated when passing through drawing rooms that were overly warm.

LYNDHURST MANSION, TARRYTOWN, NY

By the latter part of the Gilded Age, the custom began to fall out of favor as New York's population grew, making it more difficult to host and visit so many open houses. "It would be utterly impossible now when New York is so large that it would take a week of constant visiting to go through and cover the vast territory," stated a 1904 *Town and Country* article. The custom also began to have "coarse associations," as many boys and politicians used it as an excuse to drown their sorrows or celebrate their victories "in sweet champagne and new whiskey."

New Year's Eve

In the Gilded Age, ringing in the New Year was marked with similar fanfare, as it is today. In Philadelphia, bells would toll to bid "farewell to the dying year" and then turn more cheerful in tone, and there would be pistol, gun, and cannon shots to welcome the new year. These "New Year Shooters" were not necessarily appreciated by some, and an 1873 *Philadelphia Inquirer* article claimed the mayor and police tried to stop the loud reveling that year, although the shooters "evidently enjoyed themselves thoroughly and were the cause of a great deal of fun to others." They marched up and down the streets starting around 10:00 p.m. and kept up the raucous behavior all through the night into the early morning hours. There were several different groups, all wearing colorful clothing and playing brass instruments. If this sounds familiar to present-day Philadelphians, it is because these "shooters" later evolved into the Philadelphia New Years Shooters and Mummers Association (now known as the Mummers). By the 1880s, the group celebrations had grown into a more organized parade format with two main groups of participants: fancy dress clubs and comic clubs. First sponsored by the city of Philadelphia in 1901, the Mummers now have their own parade in Philadelphia on New Year's Day, complete with extravagant costumes and string bands.

New York hotels and restaurants were especially popular locations for New Year's Eve dinners and celebrations. According to a 1910 *New York Times* article, an estimated 100,000 people dined out in the city on New Year's Eve that year, which translated to a total of $1 million to cover the cost of dinners, flowers, wine, cigars, and taxicabs. Although four new restaurants had opened—the Ritz-Carlton, Rector's, the Martinique, and Louis Martin's—which helped accommodate the crowds, all restaurants were filled to capacity. The distribution of "noise-making novelties" started at 11:00 p.m., and the merriment was accompanied by orchestras, soloists, and singing quartets. Just like today, the lights were dimmed at 11:55 p.m., and corks were popped to pour champagne, with everyone clinking glasses, saying good-bye to the old year, and welcoming the new. Many wore funny hats and played tambourines, cowbells, and other instruments. Women received souvenirs such as velour purses with gold clasps, gilt bonbon boxes, gold mirrored powder cases, shiny hand mirrors, and crimson parasols. The Hotel Knickerbocker featured trumpeters in costume and boys in colonial dress, and Maxim's restaurant had a person dressed up as Father Time, complete with a scythe to "cut out" the old year, as well as a diminutive Cupid to ring in the new. Dinner included dishes such as broiled lobster and cost $5–10 a plate (about $175–$350 today).

Folks in Chicago also enjoyed ringing in the New Year in style. According to a December 1909 tongue-in-cheek *Chicago Tribune* article, restaurants that year were booked with "names from the social register," and social clubs held large dances, followed by supper gatherings "filling nearly all the rooms in their luxurious structures." Other New Year's Eve revelers preferred to "avoid the avalanche of exuberance found in the cafes and to hold private celebrations in their homes." The article estimated residents would spend a combined $500,000 on New Year's festivities that year (about $17.6 million today), including $60,000 for champagne, $25,000 for dinner parties, $20,000 for flowers, $30,000 for taxicabs, and $75,000 for tips. Other costs included items such as theater tickets, table reservation bonuses, and "toilette enhancements."

Macaroons

Macaroons are one of the oldest known cookies. When first introduced, macaroons were made by using very finely chopped almonds mixed with sugar and egg whites, almost like a marzipan. Later versions added coffee, vanilla, chocolate, cinnamon, lemon, orange, nuts, or fruit. Macaroons were featured on many New Year's Day luncheon and dinner menus in the Gilded Age, including Boston Cooking School teacher and cookbook author Mary Lincoln's "From Day to Day" column in The American Kitchen Magazine. *The following recipe uses almond paste, which can be found today in the baking aisle of many grocery stores (see photo on page XX).*

MAKES ABOUT 2 DOZEN COOKIES

One 8-ounce package almond paste (such as Solo brand)
⅔ cup superfine sugar*
1 teaspoon cake flour
2 egg whites, room temperature
Confectioners' sugar (optional)

Preheat oven to 350°F. Line two baking sheets with parchment paper.

Cut the almond paste into small pieces and place in a large mixing bowl. Sift sugar and flour and add to almond paste, mixing well using a stand or hand mixer on medium speed. Slowly add egg white until a sticky dough is formed.

Using a small cookie scoop, drop 1-inch rounds, 1 inch apart, onto baking sheets. Place on the middle and bottom racks of the oven and bake for 20 minutes. Remove from the oven and let stand for 5 minutes before detaching them from the baking sheets and moving to a wire rack. When completely cool, sprinkle with confectioners' sugar if desired.

** If you can't find superfine sugar, simply process granulated sugar for one minute in a food processor or blender.*

Almond Cakes

These delightful cupcakes were featured in an 1899 Good Housekeeping *article titled "Cakes and Dainties for New Year's Reception," by Eliza R. Parker, alongside confections including New Year's cake (a fruity cake very similar to the Christmas Cake on page 69), Neapolitan ice cream, and Macaroons (page 154). Eliza Parker was a cooking instructor, writer, and pure foods lecturer who endorsed products such as Cleveland Baking Powder, Gold Medal Flour, and Cerealine breakfast cereal. She was a frequent recipe and advice contributor to many Gilded Age ladies' magazines, as well as being the author of* Mrs. Parker's Complete Housekeeper.

MAKES 1 DOZEN CUPCAKES

1 stick (½ cup) salted butter, softened
1 cup sugar
4 eggs, separated
½ tablespoon orange flower water
½ teaspoon lemon zest
1½ cups all-purpose flour
1 teaspoon baking powder
¼ cup sliced almonds

Preheat the oven to 350°F. Line a 12-cup cupcake or muffin pan with baking papers.

Cream the butter and sugar until a pale yellow color. Add the egg yolks, orange flower water, and lemon zest until well mixed. Set aside.

In a separate bowl, whip the egg whites until soft peaks form. Mix into the other ingredients, then add flour and baking powder. Stir until just incorporated.

Spoon the batter into cupcake pan. Divide the sliced almonds among the cups.

Bake for 18–22 minutes and then put pan on a wire rack. Remove cupcakes from the pan when completely cool. Sprinkle with confectioners' sugar or garnish with an almond half and a dusting of pink decorating sugar if desired.

Sugared Fruit

In the Gilded Age, sugar was sometimes added to fruit that was not as ripe or juicy as desired. For example, tropical pineapples had to travel quite a distance to reach many American tables and could often be tough and fibrous to eat. So sometimes they were diced, covered with sugar, and placed in the center of a glass dish, with a row of sponge-cake slices or ladyfingers arranged around the sides. Other fruit, such as plums, cherries, grapes, cranberries, and currants, would be iced, made by dipping fruit pieces in beaten egg white, rolling them into finely granulated sugar, and then placing them on a sieve to dry. You can get the same effect by swapping a sugar syrup for the egg whites, as outlined here (and similar to the crystallization process used in the Gilded Age, mentioned in the sidebar below). Not only does the fruit taste delicious, but it is a festive addition to the holiday table *(see photos on pages 72 and 148).*

1 cup cranberries (or 2 cups red or green grapes)*
1½ cups sugar, divided
1 cup water

Place cranberries (or grapes) in a large, shallow heatproof dish. Set aside.

Place 1 cup sugar and water in a medium-sized pot over medium heat. Bring mixture to a boil, stirring with a wire whisk until all the sugar is dissolved. Remove from heat and allow to cool for 5 minutes. When cool, pour over the cranberries (or grapes), turning to make sure the fruit is coated with the sugar syrup on all sides. Cover and set aside for 10 minutes.

Line two large baking sheets with parchment paper. Using a slotted spoon, transfer the cranberries (or grapes) to one of the baking sheets (setting the other aside for later). Allow the fruit to dry uncovered for 1 hour, making sure none of the berries or grapes are touching. (If using grapes, you could instead arrange them on a wire rack placed over the baking sheet since they are a little larger in size.)

Pour the remaining ½ cup sugar in a large bowl or tray and then gently roll the cranberries or grapes in the sugar, using a spoon or tongs, making sure their surfaces are fully coated. Then place them on the other parchment paper–lined baking sheet and allow to dry for 1 more hour.

SUGARED FRUIT

CONTINUED

Serve immediately or store in a covered container in the refrigerator for a few days. If they appear a bit wet after storing, roll them again in a little more sugar just before serving.

** If using grapes, feel free to use a colorful mix of red and green. They can either be removed from the stem or left on the stems for a pretty presentation.*

Reproduction of a painting by the artist Cadurcis Plantagenet Ream, 1870.
SOURCE: WIKIMEDIA COMMONS.

Fruit is perhaps the oldest form of dessert. Naturally sweet and rich tasting, fruit was often featured at the end of a meal in ancient times, either fresh or dried, sometimes paired with honey, milk, or cheese dishes. When fruit was served in its whole form as a dessert in the nineteenth century, a whole set of etiquette rules developed around the most sophisticated way to eat it. As Eliza Leslie wrote in 1864, "It is very ungraceful to eat an orange at the table, unless having cut a bit off the top, you eat the inside with a teaspoon." Eventually specialized serving dishes and cutlery were introduced to make the experience easier and more elegant, such as orange cups designed to hold half an orange (similar to an egg cup or a grapefruit bowl), orange knives and peelers, and orange spoons with pointed tips. In her book *Practical Cooking and Dinner Giving* (1878), Mary F. Henderson discusses "how they eat oranges in Havana." This innovative method involved piercing a fork through the center of the orange, holding it with the left hand like a handle, then peeling the skin in strips from the top of the orange to the fork handle, leaving all the fibrous pulp on the fork.

Even though all fruits and nuts were enjoyed, some were considered more appropriate for dessert than others, based on taste, appearance, and sweetness. Nineteenth-century cookbook writer Mrs. Isabella Beeton recommended pineapples, melons, grapes, peaches, nectarines, plums, strawberries, apples, pears, oranges, almonds, raisins, figs, walnuts, filberts, medlars, cherries, and all kinds of dried fruit, together with the "most costly and *recherché* wines." And among these types of fruits, there were preferred "dessert varieties," such as Williams apples and Houghton's seedling gooseberries. According to *The American Fruit Book* (1849), "A dessert apple should be of good size, handsome form, beautiful color, fair appearance, tender, crisp, juicy, and of a rich, fine flavor."

But fruits had their seasons, so serving them fresh was not always possible depending on the time of year. Many fruits were also fragile and could spoil easily, so in the days before refrigeration, shipping and storing them was often difficult, and getting them for the holiday table could be a challenge. However, by the latter part of the Gilded Age, faster and more reliable transportation such as trains and steamships made procuring out of season produce from warmer locales easier. As a result, the fruits that show up the most often on Christmas menus from the era are oranges, apples, grapes, bananas, raisins, and figs.

Another work-around for serving fruit involved preserving it through crystallization (extracting the juice and replacing it with sugar syrup). The process involved boiling the fruit, making a sugar syrup, and then covering the fruit to allow it to absorb the sugar. When fully fermented, the fruit was removed from the syrup and rinsed with water. It could then be either glazed (dipped in thick sugar syrup and left to quickly harden) or crystallized (dipped in the same type of syrup but cooled and hardened slowly, thus causing the sugar covering the fruit to crystallize).

From Mrs. Beeton's Household Management, 1923 edition.

SOURCE: WIKIMEDIA COMMONS.

Ginger Ice Cream

When American Nancy Johnson invented an ice cream freezer for home use in 1843, crafting ice cream and other frozen desserts became much easier and more available to the masses. The following recipe was adapted from Palatable Dishes: A Practical Guide to Good Living *(1891), a cookbook that praises the virtues of this innovation, stating, "With the help of a good ice-cream freezer, a great variety of wholesome and delicious dishes may be made with very little expense and trouble." Ginger was a popular ice cream flavor during the Gilded Age, particularly during the holidays. The original recipe called for preserved ginger, but I modified it to incorporate a triple play of ginger preserves, crystallized ginger, and ground ginger, resulting in a deliciously spicy-sweet flavor and texture.*

½ cup ginger preserves*
¼ cup finely chopped crystallized ginger
1 teaspoon ground ginger
2 tablespoons lemon juice
1 tablespoon orange juice
1 cup sugar
3 cups heavy cream
2 cups whole milk

Add all ingredients to a large bowl and stir thoroughly to combine. Pour mixture into the chilled bowl of an ice cream maker and mix until frozen per ice cream maker manufacturer's instructions. Transfer to a glass bowl and store in the freezer until ready to serve.

** I used Wilkin and Sons brand.*

New Year's Games

New Year's parties often featured games, including one called Grand. Before guests arrived, the hostess would draw matching pictures (such as flowers, birds, or cats) on white paper. These were used to make large "snowballs." To play the game, each man was given two balls with corresponding pictures. The men would line up on one side of a large room with the ladies on the other, separated by a curtain. Each man would then throw one of the balls over the top of the curtain, and whichever girl caught the ball with the same design was deemed his partner.

Another game was called Jingles. One player would go into another room, while the rest of the group would decide on a word. When the person returned, the group would give them a word that rhymed with the one they had chosen, which the player would have to guess by their movements. For example, if *bat* was the chosen word, the player was told the word rhymed with *rat*, and the players would pretend to be either flying (like the animal) or hitting a ball with a baseball bat.

Chocolate Wine

Improvements in cocoa processing throughout the nineteenth century revolutionized the manufacturing of chocolate, allowing it to assume solid, liquid, and powdered forms, paving the way for all kinds of chocolate dessert possibilities. In the decades that followed, recipes for chocolate indulgences such as blancmanges, mousses, creams, cream pies, custards, puddings, soufflés, and syrups began appearing more frequently in period cookbooks. There were even several books and recipe pamphlets featuring only chocolate recipes, such as Cocoa and Chocolate: A Short History of Their Production and Use *(1886), by James McKellar Bugbee, which included recipes for both Chocolate Wine and Wine Chocolate, which it described as "an excellent winter beverage" (see photo on page 160).*

SERVES 4–6

2 cups sherry

4 ounces (1 package) unsweetened chocolate, broken into pieces

1 cup sugar

½ tablespoon cornstarch

Place all ingredients in a medium saucepan and cook over medium heat, stirring occasionally, until chocolate is melted (2–3 minutes). Turn up heat to medium-high, bring to a boil, and then turn heat to low for about 5 minutes or until thick, stirring occasionally. Cool and serve warm or at room temperature in cordial glasses. Mixture will thicken slightly upon standing, so you may have to give it a good stir before pouring.

This also makes a delicious boozy sauce to serve warm over ice cream! Refrigerate any leftovers and set out to warm to room temperature before serving, or heat gently on low heat in a pot on the stove.

Cover Your Cheese in Crystal

A cheese course, one often just described as "fromage," on Gilded Age menus was generally included at the end of elaborate or festive meals. While the selection of cheeses was important, the fromage course gave the period hostess another way in which to show off her taste, money, and expensive serving ware.

Cheese domes, two-piece serving pieces consisting of a flat underplate and a domed cover, served two functions: preventing cheese from drying out and keeping the musky cheese smells out of the dining room. During the Gilded Age, hostesses stepped up their cheese presentation game with crystal cheese domes, which allowed guests to get a glimmer of what cheese was being offered through the clear etched dome.

Cheese domes originated in England, where the musky popular Stilton cheese was kept in large ceramic-lidded crocks that were sometimes a foot in height. Later smaller, ceramic, leaded pressed glass, and crystal servers were introduced, some of which were made to match China dish sets and were often monogrammed.

The popularity of cut glass, decorated entirely by hand by use of rotating wheels, got a real boost when a number of glass producers showed their elegant wares at the 1876 Centennial Exposition in Philadelphia. Their high lead content made the glass very clear and brilliant. According to the American Cut Glass Association, the late 1800s became known as the "Brilliant Period" for glass production, and cutting shops proliferated to meet the demand for fine pieces of cut glass being sought by wealthy American households.

Cut leaded crystal or cut glass has three distinguishing characteristics, according to the Cut Glass Association: "It has a bell-like ring when gently tapped with the fingers, a clarity and brilliance unmatched by pressed or molded imitations and weight noticeably greater than the same sized piece made of unleaded glass."

But by 1897 a new molding process and acid polishing techniques began to be used, and inferior products crept onto the market. And the vogue of setting entire tables with glass was passing. The Gilded Age was truly the heyday of elegant cut glass serving pieces.

One popular entertaining guide, *Practical Cooking and Dinner Giving* by Mary Henderson, published in 1878, notes, "I consider the table ornaments in silver much less attractive than those in fancy ware . . . including cheese-plates made from Venetian glass." She added, when shopping fashionable China shops in New York, it was "difficult . . . to know what to select, there are such myriads of exquisite plates, table ornaments and fairy-land glass."

The crystal cheese domes were presented at the table, or sometimes on a trolley, where guests could select their preferred cheese. Servers then cut off wedges of cheese and offered them to guests on small serving plates.

Strong blue cheeses as well as the popular Edam, a Dutch Gouda type, were often specifically listed on fine dining menus. The Continental Pullman Dining Car menu in 1888 included Roquefort and Edam cheeses along with Bent's Crackers, a water cracker made by a commercial bakery based in Milton, Massachusetts, which produced "cold water crackers" since 1801. The company was probably most famous for selling the original hardtack crackers used by soldiers during the Civil War. The Lincoln Hotel in New York offered brie, the French soft cheese, on the menu in 1890. Another menu from 1889, from the Hotel Ponce de Leon in St. Augustine, Florida, simply offered guests "American and Foreign Cheese."

Contributed by food historian and culinary stylist Dan Macey

BIBLIOGRAPHY

A, H. "Dainty Desserts: Tested Rules for Sweets." *Pictorial Review* 2 (1906): 48–49.

Allen, Moira, ed. *A Victorian Christmas Treasury*. CreateSpace Independent Publishing Platform, 2014.

American Christmas Stories. New York: Library of America Collection, 2021.

"Among the Clubs." *Washington Post*, January 5, 1902, 15.

Ashton, Dianne. *Hanukkah in America: A History*. New York: NYU Press, 2013.

Bagnall, Laura. "Cyanotypes: The Origins of Photography." Kew Royal Botanic Gardens, February 28, 2023. https://www.kew.org/read-and-watch/cyanotype-photography.

Bix, Cynthia Overbeck. *Spending Spree: The History of American Shopping*. Minneapolis, MN: Twenty-First Century Books, 2014.

"Brooklyn Christmas Tree Society," *Brooklyn Citizen*, December 26, 1899.

Burton, Glin. "Baskets for Christmas: What to Put in Them." *Good Housekeeping*, December 8, 1888, 91.

Cahn, William. *Out of the Cracker Barrel: The Nabisco Story, from Animal Crackers to Zuzus*. New York: Simon & Schuster, 1969.

Champlin, John Denison, and Arthur E. Bostwick. *The Young Folk's Cyclopædia of Games and Sports*. 2nd ed., rev. New York: H. Holt, 1899.

Chandler, Julia Davis. "Some Christmas Fancies." *Boston Cooking School Magazine*, December 1902, 200–201.

Chase, A. W. *Dr. Chase's Third, Last and Complete Receipt Book and Household Physician, or, Practical Knowledge for the People: From the Life-Long Observations of the Author, Embracing the Choicest, Most Valuable and Entirely New Receipts in Every Department of Medicine, Mechanics, and Household Economy*. Memorial ed. Detroit: F. B. Dickerson, 1891.

Chicago Tribune. December 26, 1909, 59.

"Chocolate Cake." Accessed July 29, 2024. https://www.foodtimeline.org/foodcakes.html#chocolatecake.

"Christmas at the White House: President Cleveland's Children Have Their First Christmas Tree." *New York Times*, December 26, 1894, 3.

"Christmas Food History." Accessed July 7, 2024. https://www.foodtimeline.org/christmasfood.html.

"Christmas Stockings." *What to Eat,* December 1907, 251.

"Christmas Tables and Christmas Dishes." *Ladies' Home Journal*, December 1905, 40.

Clare, Mable. "Christmas." *Ohio Farmer,* January 14, 1882, 30.

Cotter, Holland. "Currier & Ives, as Telling as Ozzie and Harriet." *New York Times,* July 14, 1996, H33.

Cruickshank, Tom. "A Currier and Ives Christmas." *Harrowsmith Country Life* 27, no. 173 (2003): 50–51.

"Crumbs." *Good Housekeeping*, 17 (1893): 291.

Curtis Gordon, Isabel. "Toothsome Christmas Gifts." *Collier's Once a Week*, December 18, 1902, 20–21.

"Cyanotype Process." The Historic New Orleans Collection. Accessed August 30, 2024. https://www.hnoc.org/virtual/daguerreotype-digital/cyanotype-process.

"Daily Doings of the Socially Inclined." *Pittsburg Post*, December 25, 1897, 4.

Davidson, Alan. *The Oxford Companion to Food*. Edited by Tom Jaine. 3rd ed. New York: Oxford University Press, 2014.

Dawson, W. F. *Christmas, Its Origin and Associations*. London: Elliot Stock, 1902.

DeVito, Carlo. *A Mark Twain Christmas: A Journey Across Three Christmas Seasons*. Kennebunkport, ME: Cider Mill Press, 2013.

Diamond, Becky Libourel. *Mrs. Goodfellow: The Story of America's First Cooking School.* Yardley, PA: Westholme, 2012.

Diamond, Becky Libourel. *Thousand Dollar Dinner: America's First Great Cookery Challenge.* Yardley, PA: Westholme, 2015.

"Do Your Shopping Early." *Charities and the Commons: A Weekly Journal of Philanthropy and Social Advance*, December 19, 1908, 438–39.

Donnelly, Barbara J. "Blue-Plate 'Specials' Turn into Highfliers for Some Collectors." *Wall Street Journal*, December 22, 1978, 1.

Donovan, Mary Deirdre, and Culinary Institute of America. *The New Professional Chef.* 6th ed. New York: Van Nostrand Reinhold, 1996.

Emmerich, Alexander. *John Jacob Astor and the First Great American Fortune.* Jefferson, NC: McFarland, 2013.

"English Christmas Bran Pie." *American Notes and Queries: A Medium of Intercommunication for Literary Men, General Readers, Etc.*, Christmas 1891, 95.

Fletcher, Berry, and Maria Riley. *Fruit Recipes: A Manual of the Food Value of Fruits and Nine Hundred Different Ways of Using Them*. New York: Doubleday, Page, 1907.

Forbes, Bruce David. *Christmas: A Candid History*. Berkeley: University of California Press, 2007.

Frey, Jennifer. "Barnum's Circus Minimus: The Modern History of Animal Crackers." *Washington Post*, December 28, 2001, C1.

Gatewood, Willard B. *Aristocrats of Color: The Black Elite, 1880–1920*. Black Community Studies. Fayetteville: University of Arkansas Press, 2000.

"Gave Christmas Tea to Pupils." *Philadelphia Inquirer*, December 29, 1901, 26.

"General Cycling Notes." *Philadelphia Inquirer*, December 27, 1891, 8.

Gifford, Daniel. "Christmas Cards Were America's First Social Media." *Time*. December 19, 2014. https://time.com/3639925/first-social-media.

"Good Housekeeping Eclectic." *Good Housekeeping*, December 1897, 264.

"Guide to the Papers of Joseph Albree, 1842–1898," Historic Pittsburgh. Accessed September 23, 2024. https://historicpittsburgh.org/islandora/object/pitt%3AUS-QQS-MSS47/viewer.

Gulevich, Tanya. *Christmas from A to Z: History, Observances, Legends, Customs, Symbols*. Detroit: Omnigraphics, 2011.

Hale Gilman, Elizabeth. "The Christmas Dinner." *Country Life in America*, December 1904, 142–44.

Hartel, AnnaKate, and Richard W Hartel. *Food Bites: The Science of the Foods We Eat*. New York: Springer-Verlag, 2008.

"Helen Gould's Generosity: She Provides a Bounteous Christmas Dinner for Friendless Children." *Washington Post*, December 27, 1892.

"The History of the Mummers and Philadelphia Mummery." Fralinger. Accessed September 29, 2024. https://www.fralinger.org/mummers-history.

Holbrook, Weare. "Christmas Isn't in the Cards." *Washington Post*, December 10, 1939, AM4.

"Holiday Dining." The International Museum of Dinnerware Design. Accessed August 1, 2024. http://dinnerwaremuseum.org/main/holiday-dining/#:~:text=Bing%20%26%20Grondahl%20blue%20and%20white,a%20new%20design%20each%20year.

"Holiday Games." *Peterson's Magazine*, January 1883, 93.

"The Holidays." *Philadelphia Inquirer*, December 16, 1878, 4.

Hörandner, Edith. "Gingerbread." In *Encyclopedia of Food and Culture*, edited by Solomon H. Katz, 2:132–135. New York: Charles Scribner's Sons, 2003.

"Hotels to Be Filled for New Year's Eve: 100,000 Persons Expected to Make To-Night's Celebration in Restaurants Greatest in Years." *New York Times*, December 31, 1910, 6.

"How to Dine on Christmas: Menu of a Leading Chef and the Feast Miss Helen Gould's Employees Will Enjoy." *Democrat and Chronicle* (Rochester, NY), December 24, 1899, 11.

Ice-cream and Cakes: A New Collection of Standard Fresh and Original Receipts for Household and Commercial Use. New York: Scribner, 1883.

Jerman, Tom A. *Santa Claus Worldwide: A History of St. Nicholas and Other Holiday Gift-Bringers*. Jefferson, NC: McFarland, 2020.

"A Jewish View of Christmas." *New York Times*, December 29, 1889, 15.

Kansas Home For the Friendless, Leavenworth. *The Kansas Home Cook-Book: Consisting of Recipes Contributed by Ladies of Leavenworth and Other Cities and Towns*. Leavenworth: J. C. Ketcheson, 1874.

Ladies' Aid Society of the Congregational Church (Ann Arbor, Mich). *The Ann Arbor Cook Book*. Ann Arbor: University of Michigan Reprints, 2010.

Lampton, W. J. "Shop in the Morning." *New York Times*, December 8, 1908, 8.

Lehigh Burr. December 1881, 36.

"The Letter Box." *St. Nicholas* 23, pt. 2 (1896): 701–2.

Lincoln, Mrs. "From Day to Day: Department of Notes, Queries and Correspondence." *American Kitchen Magazine*, January 1899, 139–41.

Longstreet, Abby Buchanan. *Social Etiquette in New York*. New York: D. Appleton, 1883.

Macdonald, Fiona. *Christmas: A Very Peculiar History*. Luton: Andrews UK, 2012.

Meis Knupfer, Anne. "African-American Women's Clubs in Chicago, 1890 to 1920." Illinois Periodicals Online. Accessed August 25, 2024. https://www.lib.niu.edu/2003/iht1020311.html.

Miles, Clement A. *Christmas Customs and Traditions: Their History and Significance*. New York: Dover Publications, 1976.

"Miss Helen Gould's Christmas Tree." *New York Times*, December 26, 1900.

Muir, Frank. *Christmas Customs & Traditions*. New York: Taplinger Publishing, 1975.

Murray, Catherine. "Women's Clubs." In *The Encyclopedia of Greater Philadelphia*. Accessed August 25, 2024. https://philadelphiaencyclopedia.org/essays/womens-clubs.

"New Year's Eve—Chicago." *Chicago Tribune*, December 26, 1909.

Noer, Michael. "Santa Claus' First Ride." *Forbes* 156, no. 14 (1995): 346.

"On Filling Christmas Stockings." *Woman's Life*, December 15, 1900, 21, 262.

Parker, Eliza R. "Christmas Cakes." *Harper's Bazaar*, November 26, 1892, 972.

Patent, Greg. *Baking in America: Traditional and Contemporary Favorites from the Past 200 Years*. Boston: Houghton Mifflin, 2002.

"Philadelphia and Suburbs: New Year's." *Philadelphia Inquirer*, January 2, 1873, 2.

Picone, Louis. "Grover Cleveland and the First Electric Christmas Lights in the White House." Academia, 2020. https://www.academia.edu/44291040/Grover_Cleveland_and_the_First_Electric_Christmas_Lights_in_the_White_House.

"The Prang Prize Competition: Rules Governing the Awards for Christmas Card Designs." *New York Times*, November 18, 1880, 8.

Pruitt, Sarah. "Don't Forget Santa's Cookies and Milk: The History of a Popular Christmas Tradition." History, September 1, 2018. https://www.history.com/news/dont-forget-santas-cookies-and-milk-the-history-of-a-popular-christmas-tradition.

"Rauscher." *Evening Star*, March 2, 1917.

Restad, Penne L. "Gilding Christmas: Gifts, Charity, and Commerce." *Christmas in America: A History*. New York, 1997; online ed., Oxford Academic, 2011. https://doi.org/10.1093/acprof:oso/9780195109801.003.0009.

Restad, Penne L. "The American Santa Claus," *Christmas in America: A History*. New York: Oxford University Press, 1997; Oxford Academic, 2011. https://doi.org/10.1093/acprof:oso/9780195109801.003.0010.

Rollins, David. *The Christmas Journey: A Collection of Christmas Stories*. San Francisco: HarperSanFrancisco, 1996.

Rorer, S. T. "Some Good Christmas Cookies." *Ladies' Home Journal* 12 (1906): 69.

Rose, Peter G. *Delicious December: How the Dutch Brought Us Santa, Presents, and Treats: A Holiday Cookbook*. Albany, NY: Excelsior Editions, 2014.

San Francisco Public Library. "Charles Dickens' Christmas Carol: Re-issue with Critical Commentary." Special Collections, Manuscripts & Archives, December 2017.

"Sand Tarts." Accessed June 30, 2024. https://www.foodtimeline.org/foodcookies.html#sandtarts.

Schrandt, Dawn Marie. *Just Me Cookin' Cakes*. New York: iUniverse, 2003.

Sedgwick, Sara. "Some Christmas Dainties: For Old and Young, Chicken and Oyster Pie, Bakewell Pudding, Christmas Cookies, Christmas Cakes, Children's Plum Pudding, Pineapple Pudding (Frozen)." *Independent* 43 (1891). American Periodicals Series II.

Shoemaker, Alfred Lewis. *Christmas in Pennsylvania: A Folk-Cultural Study*. Mechanicsburg, PA: Stackpole Books, 1999.

Sidney, Constance. "A New Year's Party." *Good Housekeeping*, January 1905, 83.

Simon, Scott. "Opinion: Twain's 'Letter From Santa Claus,' a Gift For All Ages." NPR, December 19, 2015. https://www.npr.org/2015/12/19/460327660/twains-letter-from-santa-claus-a-gift-for-all-ages.

Sittig, Lena Wilson. *The National Cyclopaedia of American Biography*, vol. 12. New York: James T. White, 1904.

Smiley, Michele. *The Christmas Cookie Book.* New York: Houghton Mifflin, 2019.

Smith, Andrew F., ed. *The Oxford Companion to American Food and Drink*. New York: Oxford University Press, 2007.

Snider, F. L. *The Christmas Story Book: A Collection of Christmas Tales for Boys and Girls.* New York: Frederick A. Stokes, 1907.

"The Social World." *New York Times,* December 28, 1893, 5.

"Society Outside the Capital: Interesting Events and Gossip, Both at Home and Abroad, as Chronicled in the Post's Exchanges." *Washington Post*, December 18, 1909.

"The Soda Fountain." *Western Druggist* 29 (1907): 36.

Stein, Lori, and Ronald H. Isaacs. *Let's Eat: Jewish Food and Faith*. 1st ed. Lanham, MD: Rowman & Littlefield/Stackpole Books, 2018.

St. Nicholas: A Monthly Magazine for Boys and Girls. The Christmas Number: A Special Edition Containing Tales, Essays, and Poems for the Holiday Season. New York: Century, 1883.

"Story of the Week: The Christmas Fireside (for Good Little Boys and Girls) Mark Twain (1835–1910)." In *Mark Twain: Collected Tales, Sketches, Speeches, & Essays 1852–1890*. Accessed August 1, 2024. https://www.loa.org/books/80-collected-tales-sketches-speeches-amp-essays-1852-1890.

"Sugar Cookies." Accessed July 11, 2024. https://www.foodtimeline.org/foodcookies.html#sugarcookies.

Terkel, Mary. "Christmas Eve Desserts." *Chicago Daily Tribune*, December 17, 1916, 15.

"The Christmas Stocking." *New York Times*, December 26, 1883, 4.

"Turkey and Ice Cream: Hundreds of Poor Children Revel in the Good Things of Life." *Washington Post*, December 30, 1888, 5.

"A Unique Surprise Party: A Christmas Eve Entertainment in Mrs. Astor's House." *New York Times*, December 25, 1889, 8.

Valentine, Laura J., ed. *Games for Family Parties and Children*. London: Frederick Warne, 1869.

Vaughn, Carolyne. *Christmas in the American Home: How It Changed Over Time*. New York: Grove Press, 2017.

Walsh, William S. *Curiosities of Popular Customs and of Rites, Ceremonies, Observances and Miscellaneous Antiquities*. London: Gibbings, 1898.

Warren, Virginia Lee. "Dished Up by Denmark, Christmas Plates Are a Worldwide Tradition." *New York Times*, November 20, 1977, 68.

Weaver, William Woys. "Christmas." In *Encyclopedia of Food and Culture*, edited by Solomon H. Katz, 1:414–416. New York: Charles Scribner's Sons, 2003.

Weaver, William Woys, and Jerry Orabona. *The Christmas Cook: Three Centuries of American Yuletide Sweets.* New York: HarperPerennial, 1990.

Weir, Irene. "The Christmas Festival." *Perry Magazine*, December 1904, 158.

Wernecke, Herbert H. *Christmas Customs Around the World*. Philadelphia: Westminster Press, 1959.

Westcott, Edward. *The Tale of the Christmas Tree.* New York: McGraw-Hill, 1905.

Wilcox, Estelle Woods. *The New Practical Housekeeping: A Compilation of New, Choice and Carefully Tested Recipes*. Subscription ed. Minneapolis, MN: Home Publishing, 1890.

Williams, Susan, and Margaret Woodbury Strong Museum. *Savory Suppers & Fashionable Feasts: Dining in Victorian America*. New York: Pantheon Books in association with the Margaret Woodbury Strong Museum,1985.

Wilson, C. Anne. *Food & Drink in Britain: From the Stone Age to the 19th Century*. Chicago: Academy Chicago, 1973.

Wright, Julia MacNair. *Ladies' Home Cook Book: A Complete Cook Book and Manual of Household Duties*. Philadelphia: S. M. Palmer, 1896.

"Yuletide Parties in the Big Hotels: Christmas Trees and Elaborate Decorations Features of the Leading Hostelries; Many Gay Dinner Parties Reunions a Feature at the Waldorf—Some of the Guests at the Plaza, St. Regis, Astor, and Knickerbocker." *New York Times*, December 26, 1908.

RECIPE INDEX

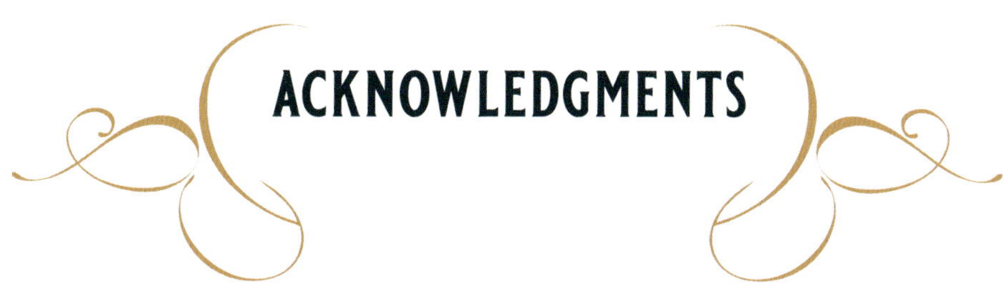

ACKNOWLEDGMENTS

This book was the culmination of the efforts and contributions of many people, and I am immensely grateful to each and every one of them. It was helpful to build off the contacts and knowledge I've gained from my prior books and experiences. I feel lucky to have made and cultivated these relationships.

Once again, I am so appreciative of Chef Walter Staib, host/executive producer of the television show *A Taste of History*; president, Concepts by Staib, Ltd.; and former proprietor of the City Tavern Restaurant in Philadelphia, who graciously wrote a lovely foreword and contributed two recipes. His German heritage and historical food knowledge aligned perfectly with the nineteenth-century Christmas themes highlighted throughout this book. Our shared admiration of culinary history is very meaningful to me, and I am grateful that we continue to grow and foster this connection though our work.

It is through Chef Staib that I was introduced to my wonderful agent, Linda Konner of Linda Konner Literary Agency. I highly value Linda's attention to detail, responsiveness, and interest in my work and look forward to working on more projects together! I also wanted to extend my sincere thanks to my editor at Globe Pequot, Greta Schmitz. Greta was supportive and enthusiastic of the concept for this cookbook from the start, and I appreciate her vision and encouragement.

I was also thrilled to once again work with photographer Heather Raub of FrontRoom Images and food historian and culinary stylist Dan Macey. Heather worked tirelessly to make sure the photographs exemplified the Gilded Age look and feel we wanted to showcase in each scene. Her ability to pivot and rise to various challenges came through over and over. We shared many laughs (and some stressful moments) over several lengthy photo sessions! Dan's food styling assistance and skilled eye on several photographs was much appreciated and brought the necessary degree of historic authenticity and design. He also generously researched and wrote several sidebars and allowed us to use many of his historic food props for the photos. I am hugely grateful for all of these contributions and highly value both Heather's and Dan's dedication, expertise, and friendship.

I also want to express my gratitude to Marisa Silva of Marisa Bakes (@marisa_bakes) for helping bake and decorate several of the cookies and other baked goods for the photos (soft molasses cookies, frosted Christmas cookies, Scotch shortbread, fudgy chocolate cake, and lemon drops). She embellished these holiday treats beautifully with her talented artistic skills, conveying the look and feel of these historic recipes, really making them pop on the page! My daughter Cate also skillfully helped create and decorate the holiday jumbles, lemon drops, and Scotch shortbread recipes. I have always been in awe of her creative abilities and very much appreciate her assistance and feedback with these decorations.

I wanted to include some authentic bonbons and chocolate candy in some of the photographs, so right away I thought of Shane Confectionery in Philadelphia, the oldest continuously run confectionery in America. Shop manager Laurel Burmeister graciously donated a box of bonbons and some chocolate bars to use in the photographs. These gorgeously decorated candies gave the photographs the perfect touch of historic accuracy.

I also wanted to acknowledge the generosity of the team at Lyndhurst Mansion in Tarrytown, New York, particularly Emma Gencarelli (film, photography, and collections coordinator), Glynis Cotton (program and events coordinator), and Krystyn Silver (associate director). They graciously gave us permission to take several photographs of the beautiful rooms at Lyndhurst, enabling us to capture the treats featured in this cookbook in an authentic Gilded Age setting that was gorgeously decorated for the holidays. It was a wonderful day, and Emma generously donated not only the space, but also her time and assistance with setting up the shots, resulting in some stunning, historically accurate photographs. I am extremely grateful to all of them!

Fellow food historian Corinne Wetzel serendipitously reached out to me about sharing some recent research on gem pans just as I was in the middle of writing this book. How ironic, since I was planning to include a recipe for spice gems! So a big thanks to Corinne and the Wagner and Griswold Society (WAGS) for allowing us to run an excerpt of Corinne's article, "Commonly Called Gem Pans: How the Gem Pan Got Its Name," which was featured in the society newsletter the *Casting Call*.

Updating all of these recipes to fit modern kitchens and ingredients requires a great deal of testing, and I am grateful to all the fellow bakers who tried them out and gave me feedback. Irene Rodgers made several recipes and kindly followed up with me by phone and email to give me specifics on how they turned out and tasted. Other recipe testers included my bestie Maria Larsen, Michele Cridland, Melinda Spink, and Karen Salomon. A big thanks to all of you for going through this process and sharing your opinions: they are greatly appreciated!

Over the course of writing the book, I also had several enthusiastic taste testers. These included my wonderful family, Joe, Cate, and Patrick, as well as our fabulous friends Bruce, Laura, India, Henry, Chris, Andy, Carol, Calli, Syd, Eileen, Kerry, Sterling, Wendy, Nancy, and John. And a big shout-out to the Poolhouse Girls: Ellen, Terri, Deb, Carolyn, and Ruthanne. All of you willingly taste-tested dozens of cookies and other baked goods and then gave me your honest feedback. In addition, many thanks to Laura for loaning some of her period china and serving pieces for the photos. It is much appreciated!

One of the huge benefits of being a food writer is the fact that I often receive cookbook donations from friends and family. I am so lucky to have added to my own collection in this way over the years. As a librarian and researcher, it is such a thrill to go through old cookbooks. Many thanks to my neighbor, Pat Johnsrud, for giving me a huge box of historical cookbooks, including gems such as *Mrs. Rorer's Every Day Menu Book* and *The Settlement Cook Book*. Heather Moran has also given me several cookbook donations during the past few years, including *Fannie Farmer's Book of Good Dinners*. And I got a huge surprise this summer when my friend Kim Whitlock gave me an 1886 copy of *The Appledore Cook Book* by Miss Maria Parloa that she got at an estate sale. She saw it and thought of me, which was so touching. My sincere gratitude to all of you for keeping me and my research in your thoughts and donations.

I also wanted to extend my sincere appreciation to my friends and family for your support! Thank you, and best wishes for a wonderful holiday season, this year and always.

ABOUT THE AUTHOR

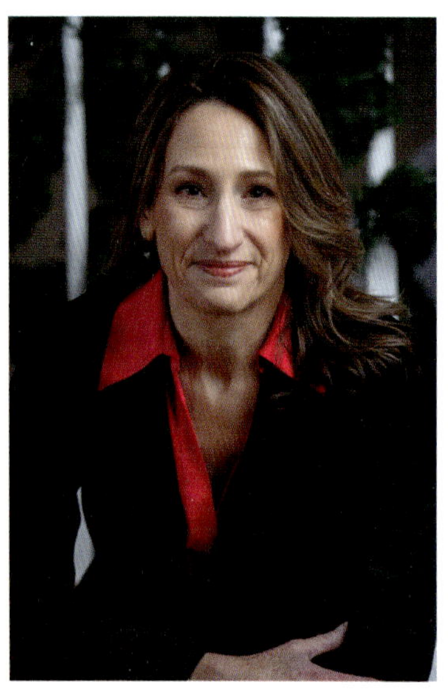

Becky Libourel Diamond is a food writer, librarian, and research historian. Her most recent book, *The Gilded Age Cookbook*, blends Gilded Age details and celebrity stories with historic menus and recipes updated for modern kitchens. She is also the author of *The Thousand Dollar Dinner* and *Mrs. Goodfellow: The Story of America's First Cooking School*. She holds a bachelor's degree in journalism from Rider University and a master's of library service degree from Rutgers University. She has worked as a business librarian at Rutgers–New Brunswick since 2020. She lives in Yardley, Pennsylvania.